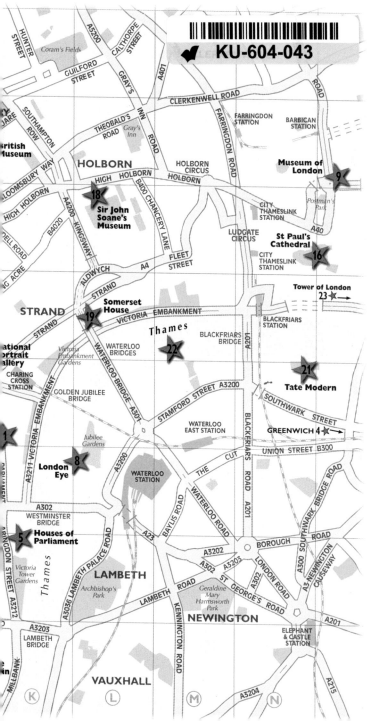

AA

CITYPACK
LONDON

TOP 25 SIGHTS AND EXPERIENCES

Contents

KEY TO SYMBOLS

- 🚼 Map reference to the accompanying pull-out map
- ✉ Address
- ☎ Telephone number
- 🕐 Opening/closing times
- 🍽 Restaurant or café
- 🚉 Nearest rail station
- Ⓜ Nearest Metro (subway) station
- 🚌 Nearest bus route

🚢 Nearest riverboat or ferry stop	🎟 Admission charges:
♿ Facilities for visitors with disabilities	Expensive (over £10), Moderate (£5–£10) and Inexpensive (under £5)
🚻 Tourist information	▷ Further information
❔ Other practical information	

Introducing London

Prepare for London to challenge your expectations. The dynamic British capital's traditions, from Savile Row outfitters to parading Horse Guards, thrive alongside a cutting-edge cultural calendar, arts venues, museums and world-class restaurants.

London buzzes with energy as whole areas of the capital have been revitalized. Spectacular modern architecture soars above ancient buildings. The cleaning of St. Paul's Cathedral has revealed its true glory; Tate Modern provides great spaces in which to enjoy contemporary art; and the Millennium Footbridge, spanning the Thames between the two sights, gives a modern edge to one of the world's best panoramic city views. Along the river, trendy restaurants fill renovated warehouses, and gardens, museums, markets, theatre and arts complexes have regenerated the South Bank.

In the redeveloped Docklands, the old Port of London is now a glittering world of skyscrapers, dominated by the innovative Canary Wharf, while construction of the Docklands Light Railway (DLR) has revolutionized the transport system. Building for the 2012 Olympic Games has transformed districts further east.

Amid all this change, the greatness of London's 2,000 years of history has not been quashed. Visitors can still roam around one of Britain's finest medieval forts, the Tower of London, or visit a real royal home, Buckingham Palace. Equally, they can picnic in one of the royal parks or take a boat ride along the Thames to evoke times when this was the backbone of London and its great port.

Londoners themselves—while appreciating their good-value theatre, free museums, great buildings and wealth of traditions—are likely to moan about just about everything else, from the high cost of property and living to the Congestion Charge and overcrowded public transport. Yet, in truth, they know they are living in the world's greatest and most vibrant city. London, the political, financial and artistic capital of Britain, is hard to beat. Everything you could ever want is here; it is up to you to take it and enjoy it.

FACTS AND FIGURES

● Greater London covers 1,584sq km (618sq miles). With a population of over 7.8 million, it is Europe's largest city.
● London is the most culturally diverse city in Britain and more than 300 languages are spoken in the capital.
● London will soon be the only city to have hosted the Summer Olympics three times (1908, 1948, 2012).

CITY WITHIN A CITY

The City of London covers about 2.5sq km (1sq mile) and is Europe's largest central business and financial district. Referred to by Londoners either as 'The City' or 'The Square Mile', it has a daily working population that swells to over 300,000. The City has its own administration and police force and every year elects its own Lord Mayor.

DOWN UNDER

The London Underground ('the Tube') is the oldest underground rail network in the world. The first line opened in 1863: 6km (4 miles) between Paddington and Farringdon Street on the Metropolitan Line. Today London Underground carries more than 1 billion passengers per year on 11 lines covering 408km (254 miles) of track and serving 27 stations.

BEATING THE COSTS

London is expensive. So, start by working out what is free. Top of the list are most major museums and galleries, the parks, monuments such as churches, and a variety of entertainment including lunch-time concerts and other events. To cut unavoidable costs, buy a Travel Pass and perhaps the London Sightseeing Pass (www.londonpass.com).

Focus On 2012 and Beyond

The regeneration of east London, with the creation of new housing, parks and sports facilities, will be the lasting legacy of London's role as host city in the 2012 Olympic and Paralympic Games.

The Promise of Regeneration

While central London received a major facelift for the Millennium and the glittering, high-rise financial hub that is Docklands has risen, phoenix-like, from the previously derelict and desolate docks, hosting the 2012 Olympics brought the opportunity to transform a socially deprived and economically depressed area in the east of the city.

London's successful bid focused heavily on urban regeneration and the promise to make the Olympic Park a blueprint for sustainable living. As a result, one of the largest urban parks in Europe is being created. Planted with native tree species and including a new wetland habitat formed from the canals and waterways of the River Lea, it links the tidal Thames Estuary and the Hertfordshire countryside.

Building on Tradition

Inspiration for this '21st-century garden city' came from London's existing city-centre parks and garden squares—think Hyde Park (▷ 71) and St. James's Park (▷ 42)—with modern versions of traditional Georgian and Victorian squares, crescents and terraces within walking distance of open spaces. Riverside properties will stretch along the banks of rejuvenated waterways. Schools, nurseries and shops, as well as faith, health and community centres, are all part of the family-focused mix.

Olympic Legacy

When the athletes and officials have left, the Athletes' Village, northeast of the Stadium, will be converted into homes, and a further five

Clockwise from top: A section of the 50-mile (80km) Lea Valley Walk; a sign for the Greenway, a traffic-free path by London's Olympic Park; an artist's impression of

distinctive new neighbourhoods with up to 8,000 homes are planned over the next 20 years.

Queen Elizabeth Olympic Park

From 2013, Londoners will be left to enjoy the former Olympic site and its facilities, which will be renamed the Queen Elizabeth Olympic Park. Attractions will include the entertainment plaza planned for the south of the park, around the Stadium; the Stadium itself, which is destined to become the new home of West Ham United football club; and the impressive Aquatics Centre, with two 50m (55-yard) swimming pools. In the north of the park, waterways, expansive parkland and green space feature and Londoners will be able to explore play areas, walking routes and cycle paths in the Lea River Valley. The Olympic Velodrome will become the hub of a new Velopark, an area including 6km (3.7 miles) of mountain-bike trails, a road-cycle circuit and off-road trails.

ArcelorMittal Orbit

ArcelorMittal Orbit, an observational tower 114m (374ft) high, designed by artist Anish Kapoor, is intended to be another lasting monument to the Games. Once it is completed, visitors to the Olympic Park will be able to climb the sculpture, a looping lattice of tubular steel, to enjoy views of the park and the London skyline from its viewing platforms.

Improved Infrastructure

The area has already benefited from the new transport links created by the Docklands Light Railway (DLR), the extended East London Line, improvements to the Underground system and better access at both Stratford International and Stratford Regional train stations, where nine rail lines link the area to central London, Britain and Europe.

ArcelorMittal Orbit; the Docklands Light Railway (DLR); a sign for the CS3 route of the Cycle Superhighway; Stratford Station, main access point to the Olympic Park

Top Tips For...

These great suggestions will help you tailor your ideal visit to London, no matter how you choose to spend your time.

...Serious Retail Therapy

Start on the ground floor of **Harrods** (▷ 124) and work up, collecting Harrods shopping bags as you go.
Be girlie: spend a whole day in **Harvey Nichols** (▷ 125) or **Selfridges** (▷ 126).
Search **Liberty** (▷ 126) for indulgent accessories.
Make a weekend foray into the five markets of the **Camden Markets** (▷ 124).
Tempt your tastebuds at **Borough Market's** (▷ 67) wonderful array of organic and artisan food stalls.

...A Meal With a View

Book a table at the **Portrait Restaurant** atop the National Portrait Gallery (▷ 150).
Rendezvous at the **Blueprint Café** (▷ 145), upstairs at the Design Museum.
Go to Canary Wharf to eat at the waterside **Gun** (▷ 147).
Splash out at **Rhodes Twenty Four** (▷ 150), with a cocktail 18 floors above at **Vertigo 42**.
Eat informally amid trees and flamingos at rooftop **Babylon** (▷ 144).

...A Breath of Fresh Air

Roam **Hampstead Heath** (▷ 77) and visit **Kenwood House** (▷ 77).
Climb high in **Greenwich Park** (▷ 20–21) to enjoy London views.
Enjoy seasonal splendour at the **Royal Botanic Gardens, Kew** (▷ 40–41).
Go boating in **Regent's Park** (▷ 72) and visit the zoo.
Do the great central London royal park walk: through **St. James's** (▷ 42–43), **Green** (▷ 70) and **Hyde parks** (▷ 71), then **Kensington Gardens** (▷ 25).

Clockwise from top: Harrods—the ultimate department store; the Great Court of the British Museum; crowds gather to watch the Changing the Guard ceremony at

...After Dark
Jazz Café, Jazz After Dark and Pizza Express Jazz Room (▷ 137) serve up quality jazz.
Check out Scala (▷ 138) and the cluster of funky clubs at King's Cross.
Dance the night away at Guanabara (▷ 135).
Barfly (▷ 133) in Camden showcases the indie scene with several acts nightly.
Head south of the river to the Ministry of Sound (▷ 136) for dependable clubbing.

...Watching the Bank Balance
Stay at funky Clink 261 (▷ 156) backpackers' hostel.
Head to Gaby's Deli (▷ 146) on Charing Cross Road for hearty, no-nonsense food.
Go to a free concert in a church such as St. Margaret, Lothbury (▷ 74).
Buy your theatre tickets at 'tkts' in Leicester Square (▷ 136).
Visit a free museum such as the British Museum (▷ 16–17).

...Peeking Inside Londoners' Homes
Dr. Johnson's house (▷ 69), where he compiled his dictionary.
Sir John Soane's two houses (▷ 48–49), filled with his antiquities.
Handel House (▷ 70), the German composer's home for 26 years.
Buckingham Palace (▷ 18–19), the Queen's London home.
Spencer House (▷ 74), the aristocratic Spencer family's mansion.

...Keeping the Kids Happy
Handle objects at the hands-on tables in the British Museum (▷ 16–17).
Climb the steps to the top of St. Paul's (▷ 44).
Go boating in Regent's Park (▷ 72).
Explore the hands-on exhibits at the Launch Pad in the Science Museum (▷ 47).

Buckingham Palace; the Making the Modern World gallery at the Science Musuem; time out in Green Park; the 19th-century Palm House at Kew Gardens

Timeline

1042 Edward the Confessor becomes king, making London the capital of England and Westminster his home; builds the abbey church of St. Peter.

1066 The Norman king, William the Conqueror, defeats King Harold at the Battle of Hastings; begins the Tower of London.

1485 Tudor rule commences, ending in 1603 with the death of Elizabeth I.

1533 Henry VIII breaks with Rome to marry Anne Boleyn; establishes the Church of England.

1649 Charles I is executed in Whitehall; the Commonwealth (1649–53) and Protectorate (1653–59) govern England until Charles II is restored to the throne in 1660.

1666 The Great Fire of London.

1759 The British Museum, London's first public museum opens.

1851 The Great Exhibition is held in Hyde Park.

1863 World's first urban underground train service opens. In 1890 the first deep-dug train runs (known as 'the Tube').

1939–45 Blitz bombings destroy a

EARLY LONDON

● Emperor Claudius invades Britain in AD43; a deep-water port, Londinium, is soon established.

● In the year 200 the Romans put a wall around Londinium, now capital of Britannia Superior; they withdraw in 410.

THE GREAT FIRE

The fire broke out at a baker's near Pudding Lane on the night of 2 September 1666. Raging for four days and nights, it destroyed four-fifths of the City of London and 13,200 homes. Sir Christopher Wren became the grand architect of the subsequent rebuilding of the city.

The London's Burning exhibit in the Museum of London depicts the devastation the fire caused

An attack by Luftwaffe bombers during the Blitz

third of the City of London and much of the docks.

1951 Festival of Britain held on the site of the South Bank arts complex.

1960s The Beatles, Carnaby Street and the King's Road help create 'swinging London'.

1981 Regeneration and development of London Docklands begins.

1994 First Eurostar trains link London and Paris through the Channel Tunnel.

1999 Ken Livingstone is elected as the first mayor of all London.

2000 Major millennium projects are completed, rejuvenating central London.

2002 Queen Elizabeth II celebrates her Golden Jubilee.

2003 Clarence House, formerly the Queen Mother's home, first opens to the public during the summer months.

2007 Eurostar trains use refurbished St. Pancras station, no longer Waterloo.

2011 Prince William and Catherine Middleton are married at Westminster Abbey.

2012 London celebrates: the city hosts the Olympic Games and marks the Queen's Diamond Jubilee.

GROWING CITY

● During the 16th century, London was Europe's fastest-growing city; its population rose from 75,000 to 200,000.
● By 1700, London was Europe's biggest and wealthiest city, with about 700,000 people.
● London's population continued to grow, from under 1 million in 1800 to 6.5 million by 1900, peaking in the 1930s and 1940s at 10 million.
● The city's population is now 7.8 million but rising.

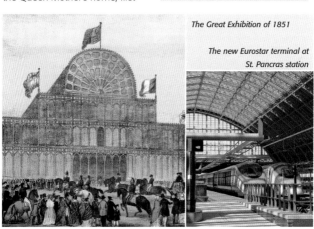

The Great Exhibition of 1851

The new Eurostar terminal at St. Pancras station

Top 25

This section contains the must-see Top 25 sights and experiences in London. They are listed alphabetically, and numbered so you can locate them on the inside front cover map.

TOP 25

HIGHLIGHTS

● Rubens ceiling
● Allegory of James I between Peace and Plenty
● Allegory of the birth and coronation of Charles I
● Weathercock put on the roof by James II
● Vaulted undercroft, a drinking den for James I
● Lunchtime concerts
● Whitehall river terrace in Embankment Gardens
● Video and self-guided audio tour

It is chilling to imagine Charles I calmly crossing the park from St. James's Palace to be beheaded outside the glorious hall built by his father. The magnificent ceiling was painted for Charles by Flemish artist Peter Paul Rubens.

Magnificent rooms This, all that remains of Whitehall Palace, was London's first building to be coated in smooth white Portland stone. Designed by Inigo Jones and built between 1619 and 1622, it marked the beginning of James I's dream to replace the original sprawling Tudor palace with a 2,000-room Palladian masterpiece. In fact, it was only the banqueting hall that was built. Inside, the King hosted small parties in the crypt and presided over lavish court ceremonies upstairs.

Clockwise from far left: The main hall, with ceiling paintings by Rubens; the elegant neoclassical exterior; a bust of Charles I, who was executed outside the Banqueting House in 1649; Rubens's nine allegorical ceiling paintings, which depict the unification of Scotland and England

Rubens ceiling The stunning ceiling was commissioned by James's son, Charles I. Painted between 1634 and 1636 by Peter Paul Rubens, the panels celebrate James I, who was also James VI of Scotland. Nine allegorical paintings show the unification of Scotland and England and the joyous benefits of wise rule. Rubens waited two years for his £3,000 fee.

The demise The palace has had a fair share of bad luck. Cardinal Thomas Wolsey lived so ostentatiously that he fell from Henry VIII's grace. Henry made it his and his successors' main London royal home. Charles I was beheaded here on 30 January 1649, and William III suffered from the dank river air. A fire in 1698 wiped out the Tudor building, leaving only the Banqueting House.

THE BASICS

www.hrp.org.uk
🕂 K6
✉ Whitehall, SW1
☎ 0844 482 7777
🕐 Mon–Sat 10–5; last admission 4.30. Closed 24 Dec–1 Jan, public hols and for functions
🚇 Westminster, Charing Cross, Embankment
♿ None
💷 Moderate
❓ Occasional lunchtime and evening concerts

HIGHLIGHTS

- Enlightenment Gallery
- Oriental antiquities
- African Galleries
- Rosetta Stone
- Living and Dying Gallery
- Elgin Marbles
- Assyrian and Egyptian rooms
- The King's Library
- Norman Foster's Great Court redevelopment

TIPS

- Pick up a plan in the Great Court and choose just a few rooms to explore.
- Take an Eye Opener tour.
- Do the Hands-On object handling.
- Rent an audio guide.

The collection at the British Museum is truly breathtaking, with a wealth of ancient treasures to see, among them bronzes from the Indian Chola dynasty and the lion-filled reliefs that once lined an Assyrian palace.

Physician founder Sir Hans Sloane, after whom Sloane Square is named, was a fashionable London physician, 'interested in the whole of human knowledge' and an avid collector of everything from plants to prints. When he died in 1753 aged 92 he left his collection of more than 80,000 objects to the nation on condition that it was given a permanent home. Thus began the British Museum, opened in 1759 in a 17th-century mansion, Britain's first public museum and now its largest, covering 5.5ha (13.5 acres), with eight million objects.

Clockwise from far left: The Queen Elizabeth II Great Court, designed by Foster and Partners as part of a redevelopment in the late 1990s; the historic circular Reading Room, at the heart of the Great Court; exhibits in the museum's Egyptian collection; the museum's imposing main entrance

Expansion George II, George III and George IV added to Sloane's collection, as did other monarchs. Their gifts, combined with the Townley and Elgin Marbles, burst the building's seams, and so architect Robert Smirke designed a new museum, completed by his son, Sydney, in 1857. Even so, with booty from expeditions and excavations pouring in, the natural history collections moved to South Kensington (▷ 36–37). When the British Library (▷ 67) moved to St. Pancras in 1998, the Great Court was redeveloped and the King's Library transformed into a gallery on the Enlightenment.

Starting to explore Head to the glass- and steel-roofed Great Court, a magnificent space with an education centre, lecture theatres, seminar rooms and cafés, to get your bearings.

THE BASICS

www.thebritishmuseum.org

🔒 J3

✉ Great Russell Street, WC1 (another entrance in Montague Place)

☎ 020 7323 8299

🎦 Galleries: Sat–Thu 10–5.30, Fri 10–8.30. Great Court: Sat–Thu 9–6, Fri 9–8.30

🍴 Restaurant, cafés

🚇 Holborn, Tottenham Court Road

♿ Very good

💷 Free, except for some temporary exhibitions

❓ Full educational schedule

17

3 Buckingham Palace

HIGHLIGHTS

● The Queen's Gallery
● Changing the Guard
● State Coach, Royal Mews
● Nash's facade,
Quadrangle
● Gobelin tapestries in the
Guard Room
● Throne Room
● Van Dyck's portrait of
Charles I and family

TIPS

● To avoid the lines, book
a timed ticket in advance.
● Visit the quality royal
souvenir shops.

Of the London houses now open to visitors,
the Queen's own home is perhaps the most
fascinating: Where else can you see a living
sovereign's private art collection, drawing
rooms and horse harnesses?

Yet another palace British sovereigns have
had homes all over London over the years;
moving from Westminster to Whitehall to
Kensington and St. James's, and finally to
Buckingham Palace. It was George III who
bought the prime-site mansion, Buckingham
House, in 1762 as a gift for his new bride, the
17-year-old Queen Charlotte, leaving St.
James's Palace to be the official royal residence.

Grand improvements King George IV and his
architect John Nash made extravagant changes

Clockwise from far left: Buckingham Palace is the London home of the British sovereign—the red, gold and blue Royal Standard is raised when the Queen is in residence; visitors at the palace gates; the Grand Staircase, designed by John Nash; the Mall, the ceremonial route to the palace

using Bath stone, later covered up by Edward Blore's façade added for Queen Victoria. Today, the 600 rooms and 16ha (40-acre) garden include the State Apartments, offices for the Royal Household, a cinema, swimming pool and the Queen's private rooms.

Open house The Queen inherited the world's finest private art collection. The Queen's Gallery, opened for her Golden Jubilee in 2002, exhibits some of her treasures. In the Royal Mews, John Nash's stables house gleaming fairy-tale coaches, harnesses and other apparel used for royal ceremonies. Don't miss the Buckingham Palace Summer Opening, when visitors can wander through the grand State Rooms resplendent with gold, pictures, porcelain, tapestries and thrones.

THE BASICS

www.royal.gov.uk

➕ G7

✉ Buckingham Gate, SW1

☎ 020 7766 7300; Queen's Gallery 020 7766 7301; Royal Mews 020 7766 7302

◉ Queen's Gallery: daily 10–5.30, last admission 4.30. Royal Mews: mid-Mar to Oct daily 11–5; Nov–22 Dec Mon–Sat 11–4; 3 Jan to mid-Mar Mon–Fri 11–4; last admission 45 min before closing. Closed Ascot week and ceremonial occasions. State Rooms, Buckingham Palace: Aug–Sep daily 9.45–6.30 (last admission 3.45)

🚇 Victoria, Hyde Park Corner

🚌 Victoria

♿ Excellent

💰 Expensive

❓ No photography

HIGHLIGHTS

- *Captain Augustus Keppel* by Sir Joshua Renolds (Queen's House)
- Maritime equipment at the National Maritime Museum
- Winter star gazing at the Royal Observatory

A UNESCO World Heritage Site, this historic London district is a highly recommended day out, enthralling children and adults with science, sea stories and an excellent art collection. The town itself has a market, restaurants and a park.

Old Royal Naval College and the *Cutty Sark* Stop first at the *Cutty Sark*, once one of the fastest tea clippers in the world. Ravaged by fire in 2007, it has taken five years to restore. Continue into the main quadrangle of the Old Royal Naval College. With your back to the Thames, the remarkable Painted Hall, notable for its spectacular ceiling, is on the right.

Art and maritime heritage At the foot of Greenwich Park, the Queen's House and

Clockwise from far left: The Royal Observatory, designed by Sir Christopher Wren; the Greenwich Meridian, the point chosen as 0° Longitude; the Cutty Sark's figurehead; the Cutty Sark; the Galvanic Magnetic Clock on the Greenwich Meridian, from which time around the world is measured

National Maritime Museum stand adjacent to each other. The Queen's House is beautifully proportioned but the real surprise is the outstanding art collection inside. The National Maritime Museum is crammed with hands-on exhibits that answer pressing questions such as why the sea is salty. Boats on display range from small dinghies to the *Miss Britain III*, the first powerboat to top 100mph. Don't miss the fascinating collection of navigational equipment.

Astronomical delights Inside Sir Christopher Wren's cramped Observatory, small galleries explain how time is measured. But the new astronomy galleries of the Planetarium next door merit much more time; they're modern, engaging and exciting but don't simplify the bigger questions about the universe.

THE BASICS

www.visitgreenwich.org.uk

Off map at S7

Greenwich, SE10

Restaurants and cafés

DLR Greenwich, Cutty Sark

Greenwich, Maze Hill

From Westminster

Old Royal Naval College and *Cutty Sark*
www.oldroyalnavalcollege.org

Grounds daily 8–6; Painted Hall, Chapel and Discover Greenwich Visitor Centre daily 10–5; last admission 30 min before closing

The Queen's House, Royal Observatory, Planetarium, National Maritime Museum

Daily 10–5; last admission 30 min before closing

HIGHLIGHTS

- View from Westminster Bridge
- Big Ben
- Summer tours
- St. Stephen's Hall
- Westminster Hall
- State Opening of Parliament
- Central Lobby

Britain is governed from this landmark building alongside the River Thames. For many visitors, its clock tower and Big Ben chiming the hour symbolize London. Interesting tours reveal its architecture, traditions and the workings of government.

Powerhouse for crown and state William the Conqueror made Westminster his seat of rule to watch over the London merchants. It was soon the heart of government for England, then for Britain, then for a globe-encircling empire. It was also the principal home of the monarchs until Henry VIII moved to Whitehall. Here the foundations of Parliament were laid according to Edward I's Model Parliament of 1295: a combination of elected citizens, lords and clergy. This developed into the House of

Clockwise from top left: A night-time view of the Houses of Parliament from the South Bank; Thomas Thornycroft's early 20th-century bronze of Boadicea by Westminster Bridge; Big Ben and the London Eye; Central Lobby, a meeting place between the House of Commons and the House of Lords

Commons (elected Members of Parliament) and the House of Lords (unelected senior members of State and Church). Henry VIII's Reformation Parliament of 1529–36 ended Church domination of Parliament and made the Commons more powerful than the Lords.

Fit for an empire Having survived the Catholic conspiracy to blow up Parliament on 5 November 1605, most of the buildings were destroyed by a fire in 1834. Kingdom and empire needed a new headquarters. With Charles Barry's plans and A.W. Pugin's detailed design, a masterpiece of Victorian Gothic was created. Behind the facade, the Lords is on the left and the Commons on the right. If Parliament is in session, there is a flag on Victoria Tower or, at night, a light on Big Ben.

THE BASICS

www.parliament.uk

⊞ K8

✉ Westminster, SW1

☎ 020 7219 3000; Commons 020 7219 4272; Lords 020 7219 3107; tours 0844 847 1672

🕐 Visits to House of Commons public gallery when house is sitting: Mon–Tue 2.30–10.30, Wed 11.30–7.30, Thu 10.30–6.30, Fri 9.30–3. Tours during summer recesses (usually Aug–Sep) and Sat throughout the year 9.15–4.40. Tours take 75 min and depart every 15 min. UK citizens can arrange tours at other times through their MP

🚇 Westminster

🚉 Waterloo

💷 Parliament free; tours expensive

❓ State Opening of Parliament mid-Nov

HIGHLIGHTS

- King's Grand Staircase
- Presence Chamber
- Wind dial, King's Gallery
- King's Drawing Room
- Princess Victoria's dolls' house
- Round Pond
- Tea in the Orangery
- Italian Gardens

One of the reasons that King William III moved out of dank Whitehall Palace and into a mansion in tiny Kensington village was that he suffered from asthma and was looking for an area with cleaner air.

Perfect location The year he became king, 1689, William and his wife Mary bought their mansion, perfectly positioned for London socializing and country living. They brought in Sir Christopher Wren and Nicholas Hawksmoor to remodel and enlarge the house, and moved in for Christmas.

A special royal home Despite the small rooms, George I introduced palatial grandeur with Colen Campbell's staircase and state rooms. Queen Anne added the Orangery (the

Clockwise from far left: A view of the palace from Dial Walk in Kensington Gardens; a statue commemorating William III, the palace's first royal resident; George Frampton's famed statue of Peter Pan in Kensington Gardens; the Orangery; the peaceful Italian Garden, a Victorian addition

architect was Nicholas Hawksmoor, the wood-carver Grinling Gibbons) and annexed a chunk of royal Hyde Park, a trick repeated by George II's wife, Queen Caroline, who created the Round Pond and Long Water to complete the 110ha (275-acre) Kensington Gardens. Today, a variety of trees are the backdrop for sculptures (George Frampton's fairytale *Peter Pan*, ▷ 72), monuments, and contemporary exhibitions at the Serpentine Gallery.

New look A £12 million project, due for completion in spring 2012, will open up previously unseen areas of the palace and create landscaped public gardens. New routes will focus on different historical eras and figures, including Diana, Princess of Wales, and Queen Victoria, whose story is told in her own words.

THE BASICS

www.hrp.org.uk

✚ A6

✉ Kensington Gardens, W8

☎ 0844 482 7777; Serpentine Gallery 020 7402 6075; www.serpentinegallery.org

🕐 Mar–Sep daily 10–6; Oct–Feb 10–5; last entry 1 hour before closing. Serpentine Gallery daily 10–6

🍴 Café, Orangery (▷ 149)

🚇 High Street Kensington, Queensway

♿ Good

💷 Expensive; family tickets. Serpentine Gallery free

❓ Personalized tours by expert Explainers

HIGHLIGHTS

● Food halls at Harrods
● Designer dresses at Harvey Nichols
● Boutiques on Walton Street

TIPS

● In Harrods, check out the day's events, shows and demos.
● If you need a special outfit, no staff are more helpful than at Harvey Nichols.
● If it rains, stay put in Harrods and visit the spa.

London's smartest and most expensive real estate conurbation, with shops and price tags to match, Knightsbridge is the place for some exhilarating retail therapy.

Stylish shops As you leave the Underground station (Sloane Street exit) you'll see Harvey Nichols (▷ 125), London's most fashionable department store. On emerging from Harvey Nichols, head back towards the Underground and continue along Brompton Road. Opposite is a huge Burberry store, known for its distinctive tan-and-grey check design. On the left as you walk towards the canopied shopfront of Harrods (▷ 124) is Swarovski, with its window displays of diamond jewellery. Leave Harrods by the Hans Road exit and you'll see lingerie store Rigby & Peller across the street.

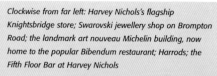

Clockwise from far left: Harvey Nichols's flagship Knightsbridge store; Swarovski jewellery shop on Brompton Road; the landmark art nouveau Michelin building, now home to the popular Bibendum restaurant; Harrods; the Fifth Floor Bar at Harvey Nichols

Even more stylish shops Return to Brompton Road and pass leather store Mulberry, before turning left into Beauchamp Place for smart restaurants, designer fashion and the Map Shop, with its precious maps and engravings. At the end of Beauchamp Place, turn right into attractive Walton Street, lined with interior design, jewellery and children's clothes shops. Ahead you'll see Joseph, which sells stylish women's clothing. With Chanel to your right across Brompton Road, turn left into Sloane Avenue by the iconic Michelin building. The Conran Shop, selling contemporary design for the home, is on the right, with fashion from Paul Smith and Joseph for Men on the left. Continue down Sloane Avenue to reach the King's Road or turn left for Sloane Square, home to Peter Jones, the department store.

THE BASICS

➕ D7–8

✉ Knightsbridge

🍴 Harvey Nichols restaurants and café-bars on the 4th and 5th floors, and a sushi bar on the 5th floor. The Caramel Room in the Berkeley Hotel (Wilton Place, tel 020 7235 6000, serves afternoon tea daily 1–6)

🚇 Knightsbridge

HIGHLIGHTS

● Panoramic views across the city in every direction
● On a clear day you can see for 40km (25 miles)
● Spotting Thames landmarks
● Aerial view of the Palace of Westminster

TIPS

● It is best to book ahead, although not essential.
● Evening riders enjoy the London lights.
● Tickets include access to the 4-D Experience, a 3-D film with special effects.

London's most visible attraction, soaring 135m (443ft) above the South Bank of the Thames, is Europe's tallest observation wheel and affords spectacular city views.

Riding high Passengers ride in one of the 32 capsules that rotate smoothly through 360 degrees in a slow-moving 30-minute flight. Each capsule is fully enclosed and comfortably holds 25 people. Because the capsules are secured on the outside of the wheel (rather than hung from it like a Ferris Wheel), views through the large glass windows are totally unobstructed. Passengers can walk freely inside the capsules, which are kept level by a motorized motion stability system—although seating is provided. Each capsule is in touch with the ground via camera and radio links. The wheel is

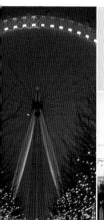

Clockwise from far left: Opened in 2000, the Eye quickly became an established part of the South Bank's landscape; the Eye at night; the glass capsules, attached to the outside of the wheel, offer unobstructed views; an aerial view of the Palace of Westminster at dusk

in constant motion, revolving continuously at 0.26m (0.85ft) per second, a quarter of the average walking speed, enabling passengers to walk straight on and off the moving capsules. After dark, the trees lining the approach to the London Eye are bathed in magical blue lights, while the boarding platform appears to float on a cloud of more blue light.

Revolutionary design Conceived by David Marks and Julia Barfield to celebrate the millennium, the Eye represents the turning of the century and is a universal and ancient symbol of regeneration. It took seven years and the expertise of people from five European countries for their design to be realized. The Eye is on the riverside Thames Path, which continues east all the way to the Thames Barrier.

THE BASICS

www.londoneye.com

➕ L7

✉ Riverside Gardens, next to County Hall, SE1

☎ 0871 781 3000; booking 0870 500 0600

🕐 Jul–Aug daily 10–9.30; Apr–Jun 10–9; Sep–Mar 10–8.30

🍴 Riverfront cafés

Ⓡ Waterloo, Westminster, Embankment, Charing Cross

🚃 Waterloo

♿ Very good. Boarding ramp available for wheelchair users

💷 Expensive

HIGHLIGHTS

- London Before London Gallery
- Hoard of 43 gold Roman coins
- Spitalfields Woman (Roman)
- Viking grave
- The lavish, late-18th-century Fanshawe dress
- Model of Tudor London
- Pleasure Gardens

A visit here is easily the best way to cruise through London's 2,000 years of history, pausing to see a Roman shoe or the Lord Mayor's State Coach, or to peek through a Victorian shop window; and it is even built on the West Gate of London's Roman fort.

A museum for London This is the world's largest and most comprehensive city museum, opened in 1976 in a building by Powell and Moya. The collection combines the old Guildhall Museum's City antiquities with the London Museum's costumes and other culturally related objects. The continuous building work and redevelopment in the City since the 1980s, allied with increased awareness about conservation, has ensured a steady flow of archaeological finds into the collection.

Clockwise from left: A window to the city's past: the lavish 18th-century Lord Mayor's State Coach on display at the museum; the original museum building, built in the 1970s; coins from the first century AD, part of the impressive Roman exhibit

MUSEUM OF LONDON

ANTONINUS PIUS
Emperor AD138–61

A museum about London The building is, appropriately, in the barbican of the Roman fort, and the rooms are laid out chronologically to keep the story clear. The London Before London gallery follows the story of prehistoric Londoners before Roman settlement. One of the most impressive galleries is Roman London, which explains the founding of Londinium in about AD50 until AD410 when the Roman army quit Britain. The Expanding City chronicles the Great Fire of 1666 to the 1850s, an era of wealth, power and global influence. People make a city, so in every room it is Londoners who are really telling the story, whether it is through Roman ceramics or Tudor clothes. A £33 million redevelopment has resulted in superb displays and a mesmerizing re-creation of the 18th-century Vauxhall Pleasure Gardens.

THE BASICS

www.museumoflondon.org.uk

➕ P3

✉ 150 London Wall, EC2

☎ 020 7001 9844

🕐 Daily 10–6; galleries begin to close at 5.40. Closed 24–26 Dec, 1 Jan

🍽 Café

🚇 Barbican, Moorgate, St. Paul's

🚉 Moorgate

♿ Excellent

🆓 Free

❓ Full education schedule; audio tour

HIGHLIGHTS

- *Virgin Enthroned*, Cenni di Peppi Cimabue
- Cartoon, Leonardo da Vinci
- *Pope Julius II*, Raphael
- *The Arnolfini Wedding*, Van Eyck
- Equestrian portrait of Charles I by Van Dyck
- *The Haywain*, John Constable
- *Madonna of the Pinks*, Raphael
- *The Archers*, Henry Raeburn
- *Sunflowers*, Van Gogh
- *Mr and Mrs William Hallett*, Gainsborough
- *La Pointe de Hève*, Monet
- Restored entrance lobby and galleries

Here is a collection of very fine pictures—and for free, so you can drop in for a few minutes' peace in front of Leonardo da Vinci's cartoon in the Sainsbury Wing or Rubens's ravishing *Samson and Delilah*.

Quality collection Founded in 1824 with just 38 pictures, the National Gallery now has over 2,300 paintings, all on show. Spread throughout William Wilkins's neoclassical building and the Sainsbury Wing extension, they provide an extremely high-quality, concise panorama of European painting from Giotto to Cézanne.

Free from the start Unusual for a national painting collection, the nucleus is not royal but the collection of John Julius Angerstein, a self-made financier. From the start it was open to

Clockwise from far left: The gallery's impressive neoclassical facade, fronting Trafalgar Square; one of the elegant galleries in the East Wing; the East Wing of the National Gallery; a detail of Vincent van Gogh's 1888 painting Sunflowers; *the exterior of the museum*

all, free of charge, and provided a wide spectrum of British painting within a European context—aims that are still maintained today. However, there may be a charge for the temporary exhibitions in the Sainsbury Wing.

A first visit To take advantage of the rich artistic panorama, choose a room from each of the four chronologically arranged sections. Early paintings by Duccio di Buoninsegna, Jan van Eyck, Piero della Francesca and others fill the Sainsbury Wing. The West Wing has 16th-century pictures, including Michelangelo's *Entombment*, while the North Wing is devoted to 17th-century artists such as Van Dyck, Rubens, Rembrandt and painters of the Dutch school. The East Wing runs from Chardin through Gainsborough to Matisse and Picasso.

THE BASICS

www.nationalgallery.org.uk

�� J6

✉ Trafalgar Square, WC2

☎ 020 7747 2885

🕙 Sat–Thu 10–6, Fri 10–9. Closed 24–26 Dec, 1 Jan

🍽 Brasserie, café

Ⓜ Charing Cross, Leicester Square

🚆 Charing Cross

♿ Excellent

💷 Free

❓ Guided tours (free daily 11.30 and 2.30, also Fri 7pm), lectures, films, audio guide, interactive screens. Free ten-minute talks (Mon–Fri 4pm), free lunchtime talks (Tue–Sat 1pm)

11 National Portrait Gallery

- *Self-portrait with Barbara Hepworth*, Ben Nicholson
- Icon-like Richard II
- The Tudor Galleries
- *Queen Victoria*, Sir George Hayter
- *The Brontë Sisters*, by their brother, Branwell Brontë
- *Isambard Kingdom Brunel*, John Callcott
- *Sir Peter Hall*, Tom Phillips
- Using the self-guiding audio tour
- An unfinished sketch of Jane Austen (c.1810) by her sister, Cassandra

It's fascinating to see what someone famous looked like and how they chose to be painted—for instance, you would never expect Francis Drake to be in red courtier's, rather than nautical clothes.

British record Founded in 1856 to collect portraits of the great and good in British life, and so inspire others to greatness, this is now the most comprehensive collection of its kind in the world, comprising oil paintings, watercolours, caricatures, silhouettes and photographs.

Start at the top The galleries, incorporating the Ondaatje Wing, are arranged chronologically, starting on the second floor—reached by stairs or elevator. Tudor monarchs kick off a visual *Who's Who* of British history that moves

Clockwise from far left: The main entrance to the National Portrait Gallery; the Tudor Galleries; portraits and busts from the Regency period on display in the acclaimed Weldon Galleries; an 1834 portrait of the Brontë sisters by their brother, Branwell; a mosaic at the museum entrance

through inventors, merchants, explorers and empire builders to modern politicians. Here you'll find Isambard K. Brunel, Robert Clive and Warren Hastings of India, Winston Churchill and Margaret Thatcher. There is Chaucer in his floppy hat, Kipling at his desk and A.A. Milne with his fictional creations Christopher Robin and Winnie-the-Pooh on his knee. Lesser-known sitters also merit a close look, such as the 18th-century portrait of the extensive Sharp Family, who formed an orchestra and played at Fulham every Sunday.

Modern times The Victorians insisted on entry only after death, but this rule has been revised. Among the many contemporary portraits, you may find those of footballer David Beckham, and ex-Beatle Sir Paul McCartney.

THE BASICS

www.npg.org.uk

➕ J5

✉ St. Martin's Place, WC2

☎ 020 7306 0055

🕐 Sat–Wed 10–6, Thu–Fri 10–9. Closed 24–26 Dec, Good Fri

🍴 Café, rooftop restaurant

🚇 Leicester Square, Charing Cross

🚆 Charing Cross

♿ Good

🎫 Free except for special exhibitions

❓ Lectures, events

HIGHLIGHTS

● Giant Earth sculpture
● Dinosaur skeletons
● Fossilized frogs
● The Vault, a gallery of crystals, gems and meteorites
● Restless Surface Gallery
● Tank Room in the Darwin Centre

TIPS

● Use the side entrance on Exhibition Road.
● The museum is huge: Plan your visit carefully.

The museum building looks like a Romanesque cathedral and is wittily decorated with a zoo of animals to match its contents: extant animals on the west side, extinct ones on the east side.

Two museums in one Overflowing the British Museum, the Life Galleries were moved here in 1880. They tell the story of life on earth. The story of the earth itself is told in the Earth Galleries, beginning with a 300-million-year-old fossil of a fern. The Darwin Centre uses IT to make the most of the museum's 70 million objects and make the work of its 300 or so scientists accessible worldwide. Take the glass lift to its futuristic Cocoon building, then wend your way down its sloping walkways, taking in the exciting insect and plant displays.

Clockwise from far left: The museum's cavernous entrance hall; the escalator leading to the Red Zone, where galleries explore the nature of the Earth; insect specimens on display at Cocoon, part of the Darwin Centre; the original 1880 Waterhouse Building

Follow the zone Colour-coded zones help you plan your visit. In the Red Zone, dramatic sculptures and a giant metallic globe lead to galleries revealing how the planet has evolved: a treasury of minerals, gems and rocks; displays on how volcanoes and earthquakes happen; and the effect of man on nature. Exhibits in the Green Zone go from dinosaurs to birds and insects via fossils and our human ancestors. The Blue Zone celebrates the amazing diversity of our planet as it explores fish, amphibians and reptiles; investigates human biology; and gets up close to the blue whale, the largest creature on Earth. Don't miss the new Images of Nature gallery, at the end of the Blue Zone, which houses a stunning collection of art inspired by nature. The superb Darwin Centre and quiet wildlife garden occupy the Orange Zone.

THE BASICS

www.nhm.ac.uk

➕ B8

✉ Cromwell Road, SW7; also entrance on Exhibition Road

☎ 020 7942 5000

🕐 Daily 10–5.50. Closed 24–26 Dec

🍴 Meals, snacks, deli café, picnic areas

🚇 South Kensington

♿ Excellent

🎟 Free; charge for some temporary exhibitions

❓ Regular tours, lectures, films, workshops

13 Portobello Road Market

- Red Lion Antiques Arcade, where it all began
- Spooky stuffed animals sold in Natural History
- The clocks and watches in Admiral Vernon arcade
- Arts and Crafts and art deco in the Crown Arcade

TIPS

- Saturday is by far the best day, when the antiques dealers set up stalls in the street.
- No price is totally fixed; bargain hard.
- It is true that the early bird finds the best prices.
- Join locals buying a treat at Tom's Delicatessen on Westbourne Grove.

Spend a Saturday wandering down Portobello Road, peering at the stalls and dipping into the shops behind them to seek out a special piece of china, a fascinating piece of glass or a pretty piece of jewellery.

Portobello Road Originally a lane leading down to Porto Bella Farm, this road has been a market site for over a century. Gypsies traded horses and herbs here in the 1870s, but the antiques dealers only arrived in the late 1940s. Today, Portobello Road Market boasts of being the world's largest antiques market. It is really a series of markets that spill into surrounding streets where almost everything imaginable is sold. If you want a day-long party of fascination, fun and friendliness, come here on any Saturday.

Clockwise from left: Antiques arcades and galleries line Portobello Road; the Saturday-morning antiques market, when antiques traders and bargain-hunters crowd the area, sees Portobello Road at its busiest; fruit and vegetables are sold in the market's lower reaches

More than just stalls Starting at the top, there are the established specialist antiques shops for maps, silver, medals and collectables, where bargains are few. Don't miss Lipka arcade and the 20th Century theatre, opposite. Farther down, where the stalls begin, the stock is more varied and visitors join locals in the pubs and cafés to discuss values and possible acquisitions. Here you find antique clothes, records and china next to contemporary ceramics and jewellery. Explore the by-roads, too.

For something different After the vegetable and organic food stalls you go under the Westway flyover and find restorative cafés. The tone changes. Here, look for funky bric-a-brac, cutting-edge street fashion, vintage clothes and even second-hand bicycles.

THE BASICS

www.portobelloroad.co.uk
➕ Off map at A5
✉ Market Office:
72 Tavistock Road, W11
🕐 Mon–Wed 9–6,
Thu 9–1, Fri–Sat 9–7
🚇 Notting Hill Gate

★14 Royal Botanic Gardens, Kew

TIP

● Take the Kew Explorer, a train that tours all the key sites in 40 minutes. Tickets are £4, available from any entrance gate, from 11am.

Whether shrouded in winter mists, bursting with azalea and rhododendron blossoms or crowded with summer picnickers, Kew Gardens are a truly magical place.

Royal beginnings The 120ha (300-acre) gardens, containing 44,000 different plants and many glorious greenhouses, make up the world's foremost botanical research centre. It began modestly: George III's mother, Princess Augusta, planted 4ha (9 acres) around tiny Kew Palace in 1759, helped by gardener William Aiton and botanist Lord Bute. Architect Sir William Chambers built the Pagoda, Orangery, Ruined Arch and three temples. George III later enlarged the gardens and Sir Joseph Banks (head gardener 1772–1819) planted them with specimens from all over the world.

Clockwise from far left: The spectacular 19th-century Palm House; a rare flowering of the gigantic titum arum in the Prince of Wales Conservatory; Kew Palace; the Nosegay Garden, filled with aromatic plants; artist Tom Hare's willow sculpture of a star anise seed on the Seed Walk

Victorian order When the gardens were given to the nation in 1841, Sir William Hooker became director. He founded the Department of Economic Botany, the museums, the Herbarium and the Library, while W.A. Nesfield laid out the lake, pond and the four great vistas: Pagoda Vista, Broad Walk, Holly Walk and Cedar Vista. The 200m (219-yard) Xstrata Treetop Walkway, which opened in 2008, offers bird's-eye views of the gardens and London skyline.

The greenhouses Chambers' Orangery (1761) is now a restaurant. Decimus Burton designed the Palm House (1844–48) and Temperate House (1860–62), which preserves some plants that are extinct in their countries of origin. See too the Waterlily House (1852) and the Princess of Wales Conservatory (1987).

THE BASICS

www.kew.org

➕ Off map at A9

✉ Kew Road, Kew

☎ 020 8332 5655

🕐 Daily from 9.30am; closing time varies

🍴 Restaurants, cafés

Ⓠ Kew Garden

🚇 Kew Bridge

🚢 Kew Pier

♿ Excellent

💷 Expensive

❓ Guided tours daily at 11, 12, 2 from Victoria Plaza (free, but register 15 min before tour starts)

HIGHLIGHTS

- Springtime daffodils
- Whitehall views from the lake bridge
- Feeding the pelicans, daily 2.30–3.30
- Views to Buckingham Palace
- Exotic plants in the tropical border

TIPS

- Inn the Park café opens early and closes late.
- It's the perfect setting for summer picnics.
- There are free concerts on summer weekends.

Drop in to St. James's Park to eat a sandwich and laze on a deckchair while listening to the band's music; try spotting palaces across the duck-filled lake and over the tips of the weeping willows.

Royal heart St. James's Park is the oldest and most royal of London's nine royal parks, surrounded by the Palace of Westminster, St. James's Palace, Buckingham Palace and the remains of Whitehall Palace. Kings and their courtiers have been frolicking here since 1532, when Henry VIII laid out a deer park in on what was then marshy water meadow and built a hunting lodge that became St. James's Palace. In the early 17th century, James I began the menagerie, including crocodiles, and an elephant who drank a gallon of wine daily.

Left: With Buckingham Palace at its western end and the Houses of Parliament within easy reach, the park is a popular retreat for visitors; middle: A drinking fountain; right: Springtime, when the daffodils are in bloom, is one of the best times to visit

French order In the mid-17th century, Charles II, influenced by Versailles, near Paris, redesigned the park to include a canal, Birdcage Walk (where he kept aviaries) and the gravelled Mall, where he played pell mell, a game similar to croquet. George IV, helped by John Nash and influenced by Humphrey Repton, softened the formal French lines into the English style in the 19th century, making this 37ha (93-acre) park of blossoming shrubs and curving paths popular with romantics.

Nature As the park is an important migration point and breeding area for birds, two full-time ornithologists look after up to 1,000 birds from more than 45 species. Pelicans live on Duck Island, a tradition begun when the Russian Ambassador gave some to Charles II.

THE BASICS

www.royalparks.gov.uk

✚ J7

✉ The Mall, SW1

☎ 020 7930 1793

🕐 Daily 5am–midnight

🍴 Inn in the Park (▷ 148)

🚇 St. James's Park, Green Park, or Westminster

🚊 Victoria

♿ Very good

💷 Free

❓ Changing the Guard (on Horseguards Parade). Bird talks; guided walks

HIGHLIGHTS

- Sung evensong
- Frescoes and mosaics
- Wren's Great Model in the Triforium (upstairs)
- Triple-layered dome weighing 76,000 tons
- Jean Tijou's wrought-iron sanctuary gates
- Wellington's memorial
- *Light of the World*, Holman Hunt
- The view across London
- Wren's epitaph under the dome

To slip into St. Paul's for evensong, and sit gazing up at the mosaics as the choir's voices soar, is to enjoy a moment of absolute peace and beauty. Go early or late to avoid the crowds.

Wren's London After the restoration of the monarchy in 1660, artistic patronage bloomed under Charles II. Following the Great Fire of London in 1666, which destroyed four-fifths of the City, Christopher Wren took main stage as King's Surveyor-General. The spires and steeples of his 51 churches, of which 23 still stand, surrounded his masterpiece, St. Paul's.

The fourth St. Paul's This cathedral church for the diocese of London was founded in AD604 by King Ethelbert of Kent. The first three

Clockwise from far left: The view of St. Paul's Cathedral from Festival Gardens; the interior of the magnificent dome, decorated with frescoes by Sir James Thornhill; the choir stalls and high altar; St. Paul's before the Fire of London in 1666; architect Sir Christopher Wren

To West View of S.t Pauls Cathedral before the Fire of London.

churches burned down. Wren's, built in stone and paid for with a special coal tax, was the first English cathedral built by a single architect, the only one with a dome, and the only one in the English baroque style. A £40 million cleaning-and-repair project marked the cathedral's 300th anniversary in 2010. Statues and memorials of Britain's famous crowd the interior and crypt—heroes Wellington and Nelson, artists Turner and Reynolds, and Wren himself.

The climb The 528 steps to the Golden Gallery at the top are worth the effort. Shallow steps rise to the Whispering Gallery for views of Sir James Thornhill's dome, decorated with frescoes and 19th-century mosaics. For virtual access to the dome, visit Oculus, a 270-degree film experience in the crypt.

THE BASICS

www.stpauls.co.uk

✚ N4

✉ Ludgate Hill, EC4

☎ 020 7236 4128

🕐 Mon–Sat 8.30–4. Galleries and Oculus: 9.30–4.15. Services include Mon–Sat 5, Sun 10.15, 11.30, 3.15

🍴 Restaurant, café

Ⓢ St. Paul's

🚆 City Thameslink

♿ Very good

💷 Expensive

❓ Multimedia, audio and guided tours included; organ recitals

HIGHLIGHTS

● Demonstrations
● Launch Pad's interactive exhibits and shows
● The glass bridge in the Challenge of Materials
● Pattern Pod, the hands-on gallery for children aged 5–8
● Atmosphere Gallery
● Puffing Billy
● 18th-century watches and clocks

TIP

● Head for the higher, quieter floors to escape the crowds.

Even if you are no scientist, it's thrilling to understand how a plane flies, how Newton's reflecting telescope worked, or how we receive satellite television. You'll find the answers using interactive exhibits. This is science at its most accessible.

Industry and science Opened in 1857, this museum comes closest to fulfilling Prince Albert's educational aims when he founded the South Kensington Museums after the Great Exhibition of 1851. Its full title is the National Museum of Science and Industry. Over the seven floors, which contain more than 60 collections, the story of human industry, discovery and invention is recounted through various tools and products, from exquisite Georgian cabinets to a satellite launcher.

Clockwise from far left: Landmark designs are displayed in the Making the Modern World gallery; displays in the Who Am I? gallery explore the wonders of human genetics and intelligence; one of the child-friendly exhibits in the Launchpad; an early 20th-century engine in the Energy Hall

Science made fun See how vital everyday objects were invented and then developed for use in Making the Modern World; find out what makes you smarter than a chimp in Who Am I?; and get involved in the very latest scientific hot topics in Antenna. The galleries vary from rooms of beautiful 18th-century objects to an astronaut's moon capsule and in-depth explanations of abstract concepts. You can even learn the basic principles of flying by testing out the hands-on equipment in the Flight gallery. Health Matters reveals how technology has dramatically changed medicine. The interactive Challenge of Materials and the high-tech Launch Pad, a favourite with children, explore science, technology and the complex world, while the Atmosphere gallery tackles climate science brilliantly.

THE BASICS

www.sciencemuseum.org.uk

🔢 C8

✉ Exhibition Road, SW7

☎ 0870 870 4868

🕐 Daily 10–6

🍴 Restaurants, cafés, picnic area in basement

🚇 South Kensington

♿ Excellent (tel helpline 020 7942 4446)

💷 Free; IMAX cinema expensive; Virtual Voyager moderate

❓ Guided tours, demonstrations, historic characters, lectures, films, workshops

TIPS

● The museum is not suitable for children.
● Atmospheric candlelit evening openings are held monthly.
● Tours are on Saturday at 11am (inexpensive).

As you move about the gloriously over-furnished rooms of Soane's two houses and into the calm upstairs drawing room, his presence is so strong and his genius so pervasive that you feel you would not be surprised if he were there to greet you.

The architect This double treasure-house in leafy Lincoln's Inn Fields, central London's largest square, is where the neoclassical architect Sir John Soane lived. First he designed No. 12 and lived there from 1792. Then he bought No. 13 next door, rebuilt it with cunningly proportioned rooms, and lived there from 1813 until his death in 1837. Meanwhile, he also designed Holy Trinity church on Marylebone Road (1824–48), and parts of the Treasury, Whitehall. His model for his

Clockwise from far left: Sir John Soane remodelled two adjoining houses to create his home in Lincoln's Inn Fields; the Breakfast Room, hung with three paintings by Canaletto—among the museum's treasures; one of the first-floor entertaining rooms; part of Soane's eclectic collection

masterpiece, the (destroyed) Bank of England, is here (recreated rooms now form part of the bank's museum, ▷ 66). No. 14 is now an area for Adam Studies.

The collector Soane was an avid collector. He found that every art object could inspire his work, so his rooms were a visual reference library. Hogarth's paintings unfold from the walls in layers. There are so many sculptures, paintings and antiquities that unless you keep your eyes peeled you are likely to miss a Watteau drawing or something better.

Opening up the Soane The project to restore the museum to its appearance at the time of Sir John's death is ongoing. The first phase is scheduled for completion in summer 2012.

THE BASICS

www.soane.org

➕ L4

✉ 13 Lincoln's Inn Fields, WC2

☎ 020 7440 4263

🕐 Tue–Sat 10–5 (also first Tue of month 6–9pm). Closed 24–26 Dec, 1 Jan, Good Fri

🚇 Holborn, Chancery Lane

🚆 Farringdon

♿ Call in advance

💷 Free (donation)

❓ Free audio tours

HIGHLIGHTS

- Courtauld Collection:
- The Fridart Collection
- *A Bar at the Folies-Bergère*, Manet
- Rubens paintings
- *The Trinity*, Botticelli

Somerset House was transformed from a lavish but forgotten building into a riverside palace. Spend some time here and enjoy French Impressionist masterpieces, summer concerts and dancing fountains.

Palatial home A majestic triple-arch gateway leads from the Strand into Sir William Chambers' English Palladian government offices (1776–86). The Courtauld Collection is housed in rooms lavishly decorated for the Royal Academy, before its move to Piccadilly. Ahead, the great courtyard has fountains, a theatre, an ice-rink and café tables, according to the season. A superb café and fine dining restaurant on the summer terrace, with Thames views, opened in 2010. Changing exhibitions are held in the Embankment Gallery.

Clockwise from far left: The courtyard of Somerset House; artistic treasures on display in the Courtauld Gallery; the Courtauld's lavishly decorated rooms, which were originally used by the Royal Academy; the elegant staircase leading to the upper floors of the Courtauld Gallery

Courtauld Gallery Industrialist Samuel Courtauld's collection of French Impressionist and post-Impressionist paintings, with works by Renoir, Cézanne, Van Gogh, Manet, Seurat and Gauguin, are on display. There are also 18th-century portraits by Goya and Gainsborough; canvases and sketches by Rubens; works by Botticelli and Tintoretto; and an important Gothic and medieval collection. Twentieth-century highlights include works by Matisse, Dufy, Kandinsky and the Bloomsbury group.

Drawings, prints and sculpture The excellent collection of prints includes works by Michelangelo, Dürer and Leonardo da Vinci, while its sculpture collection spans antiquity to the 20th century. The decorative arts are represented by fine Islamic ceramics and metalwork.

THE BASICS

www.somersethouse.org.uk
✚ L5
✉ Somerset House, Strand, WC2
☎ 020 7845 4600
🕐 Daily 10–6; extended hours for Courtyard, River Terrace and restaurant
🍴 Cafés, restaurant
🚇 Temple (closed Sun)
🚃 Blackfriars, Charing Cross
♿ Excellent
🎟 Somerset House free; Courtauld Gallery moderate, Mon 10–2 free
❓ Free guided tours of Somerset House Thu 1.15, 2.45, Sat 12.15, 1.15, 2.15 and 3.15. Tickets available from 10.30am from the information desk in the Seaman's Hall, South Building

HIGHLIGHTS

- The Clore Gallery
- Thomas Gainsborough portrait
- *Flatford Mill*, Constable
- A William Blake vision
- A William Hogarth caricature
- A Barbara Hepworth stone or wood sculpture
- A work on paper by David Hockney
- *The Opening of Waterloo Bridge*, Constable
- Temporary exhibitions
- The Tate to Tate ferry

Moving through the galleries past Gainsborough portraits, Turner landscapes and Hepworth sculptures, this is an intimate social history of Britain told by its artists.

Two for one The Tate Gallery was opened in 1897, named after the sugar millionaire Henry Tate, who paid for the core building and donated his Victorian pictures to put inside it. In 2000, the Tate's international modern art collection moved to Tate Modern (▷ 54–55), housed in the former Bankside Power Station. The national collection, renamed Tate Britain, remained in Henry Tate's original building on Millbank, and now fills the refurbished gallery.

British art The galleries are helpfully divided into four chronological suites. You can follow

Clockwise from far left: The imposing Millbank entrance to Tate Britain; paintings on display in the gallery; the rotunda dome, a masterpiece of Victorian architecture; the Turner Collection, the largest collection of works by J.M.W. Turner in the world, is housed in the modern Clore Gallery

the visual story of British art from 1500 until the present day. Although paintings, sculptures, installations and works in other media will be changed regularly, you may well see Van Dyck's lavish portraits of the 17th-century British aristocracy, William Hogarth's prints and richly coloured Pre-Raphaelite canvases. Do not miss the great Turner collection housed in the adjoining Clore Gallery.

Turner Prize Britain's most prestigious and controversial prize to celebrate young British talent is run by the Tate and awarded each autumn following an exhibition of nominees' works. Founded in 1984, winners have included Damien Hurst, Grayson Perry and Chris Ofili, while Tracey Emin, Sam Taylor-Wood and Tony Cragg have all been nominees.

THE BASICS

www.tate.org.uk

🕂 J9

✉ Millbank, SW1; entrances on Millbank and Atterbury Street

☎ 020 7887 8888

🕐 Daily 10–6. First Fri in month 10–10

🍽 Restaurant, café

🚇 Pimlico, Vauxhall, Westminster

🚉 Victoria

🚹 Very good

🎟 Free except for special exhibitions

❓ Full education schedule; audio tours

HIGHLIGHTS

Although diplays change, look out for works by:

- Pablo Picasso
- Claude Monet
- Henri Matisse
- Constantin Brancusi
- Jackson Pollock
- Mark Rothko
- Bridget Riley
- Marcel Duchamp
- Andy Warhol

The national collection of modern art fills the magnificent spaces of George Gilbert Scott's monumental Bankside Power Station by the Thames, making it a radical focus for the long strip of riverside arts emporia.

World-class art On a par with the Metropolitan Museum of Modern Art in New York, the collection that once shared space with the Tate's British collection (▷ 52–53) now blossoms in its own huge spaces. Swiss architects Herzog & de Meuron have created an exciting contemporary structure within the handsome brick building, making it ideal for exhibiting large-scale works of art in an innovative way. Gallery events, cafés, a big shop and a rooftop restaurant complete the total package for a great day on the South Bank or, using the

Clockwise from far left: The monumental Turbine Hall, used for temporary exhibitions; the Millennium Bridge, linking Tate Modern with the City; a computer-generated image of the new extension to Tate Modern; The Kiss (1901–1904) by Auguste Rodin; Claude Monet's Water-lilies (c.1916)

Millennium Bridge designed by Caro and Rogers, in a combination with City sightseeing.

20th century and more The most influential artists of the 20th century are all represented, including Picasso, Matisse, Dalí, Duchamp, Rodin, Klee and Warhol—as well as British artists such as Bacon, Hepworth, Hockney and Nicholson. Together they represent all the major periods and movements in 20th-century art. Suites of rooms, each devoted to one subject, mix together pieces from various periods.

Tate Modern project A striking new building rising behind the power station will transform the galleries, doubling the space for installation and performance art. It is scheduled for completion in 2012.

THE BASICS

www.tate.org.uk

➕ N6

✉ Bankside, SE1

☎ 020 7887 8888

🕐 Sun–Thu 10–6, Fri–Sat 10–10

🍴 Cafés, restaurant

Ⓡ Blackfriars, Southwark

🚉 Blackfriars, London Bridge

♿ Very good

🎫 Free, charge for some special exhibitions

❓ Full educational schedule. Choice of free daily audio tours

HIGHLIGHTS

● Lambeth Palace
● Houses of Parliament
● London Eye
● St. Paul's Cathedral
● Tower Bridge
● Tower of London
● Thames Barrier

TIPS

● Shop around for the best deals.
● The Tate Boat plies between the two galleries.
● Take a jacket; London weather changes quickly

A cruise along the Thames is a leisurely way to see the city. It gives a new perspective to London's development and history, which is inextricably linked with this great river.

Wonderful sights Many companies run river cruises and water-buses on the river. A particularly good stretch is from Westminster Pier in an easterly direction, which takes in a host of sights. This marks the point where the river enters central London and becomes a working highway, until recently lined with shipping, docks and warehouses. At this point the Thames flows between Lambeth Palace and the Houses of Parliament (▷ 22–23) and past the London Eye (▷ 28–29) and the Southbank arts complex, making a northern loop past the Victoria Embankment and towards the

Clockwise from top left: A view over the Thames to St. Paul's Cathedral and the high-rises of the City; amphibious craft (DUKWs) provide tours with a difference (see panel, page 167); the landmark Tower Bridge; Big Ben and the Houses of Parliament; the Thames Flood Barrier

Millennium Bridge, linking St. Paul's Cathedral (▷ 44–45) and Tate Modern (▷ 54–55).

Great bridges Beyond Shakespeare's Globe (▷ 139) and Southwark Cathedral (▷ 74) the river reaches London Bridge, the modern crossing that replaced the 1831 version, itself replacing its arched medieval predecessor. The next crossing is Tower Bridge, designed to allow tall ships passage between the city and the sea. On the north bank is the Tower of London (▷ 58–59), William the Conqueror's fort placed strategically to protect the port.

Modern versus maritime From here the river passes the redeveloped Docklands. Seafaring is the theme as the Thames reaches Greenwich (▷ 20–21) and then the Thames Barrier.

THE BASICS

⊞ K7
✉ Start point: Westminster Pier
🚇 Westminster
🚢 **Circular Cruise Westminster**
✉ 020 7936 2033; www.crownriver.com
City Cruises
✉ 020 7740 0400; www.citycruises.com
Thames River Services
020 7930 4097; www. westminsterpier.co.uk
Westminster Passenger Service Association
✉ 020 7930 2062; www.wpsa.co.uk
🎫 Moderate

TOP 25

HIGHLIGHTS

- Medieval Palace
- Raleigh's room
- Imperial State Crown
- Tower ravens
- Grand Punch Bowl, 1829
- St. John's Chapel

TIPS

- For advance tickets call 0844 482 7799 (44 20 3166 6000 from outside the UK). Alternatively, buy them online at www.hrp.org.uk.
- If buying tickets on the day, it's vital to arrive early to avoid lines.

The restored rooms of Edward I's 13th-century palace bring the Tower alive as the royal palace and place of pageantry it was; the Crown Jewels are simply priceless.

Medieval glory The Tower of London is Britain's best medieval fortress. William the Conqueror (1066–87) began it as a show of brute force and Edward I (1272–1307) completed it. William's Caen stone White Tower, built within old Roman walls, was an excellent defence: It was 27m (90ft) high, with walls 4.5m (15ft) thick, and space for soldiers, servants and nobles. Henry III began the Inner Wall, the moat, his own watergate—and the royal zoo. Edward I built the Outer Wall, several towers and Traitor's Gate, and moved the Mint and Crown Jewels here.

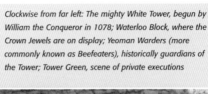

Clockwise from far left: The mighty White Tower, begun by William the Conqueror in 1078; Waterloo Block, where the Crown Jewels are on display; Yeoman Warders (more commonly known as Beefeaters), historically guardians of the Tower; Tower Green, scene of private executions

Wonder and horror Stephen (1135–54) was the first king to live here, James I (1603–25) the last. From here Edward I went in procession to his coronation and Henry VIII paraded through the city bedecked in cloth of gold. The Barons seized the Tower to force King John to put his seal to the Magna Carta in 1215; and two princes were murdered while their uncle was being crowned Richard III. Since 1485 it has been guarded by Yeoman Warders or 'Beefeaters', who also now give guided tours.

Centuries of history The Tower has been palace, fortress, state prison and execution site and its gates are still locked every night. If the history is overwhelming there is help: a good welcome area, jolly guided tours, a serious audio tour and numerous interactive displays.

THE BASICS

www.hrp.org.uk

⊞ S5

✉ Tower Hill, EC3

☎ 0844 482 7777

🕐 Mar–Oct Tue–Sat 9–5.30, Sun–Mon 10–5.30; Nov–Feb Tue–Sat 9–4.30, Sun–Mon 10–4.30

🍴 Cafés, restaurant

🚇 Tower Hill

🚉 Fenchurch Street, London Bridge, Docklands Light Railway (Tower Gateway)

♿ Excellent for Jewel House

💰 Expensive

❓ Free guided tours every 30 min; audio tours

HIGHLIGHTS

- British Galleries
- India and Islamic Galleries
- Jewellery Gallery
- Glass Gallery
- Leonardo da Vinci notebooks
- Silver collection
- Raphael Gallery
- Architecture Gallery
- The Hereford Screen

TIPS

- Hang out in the courtyard.
- Join a gallery tour or talk.
- Evening openings have a good atmosphere.

Part of the Victoria and Albert Museum's glory is that each room is unexpected; it may contain a French boudoir, plaster casts of classical sculptures, antique silver or exquisite contemporary glass.

A vision The V&A started as the South Kensington Museum. It was Prince Albert's vision: arts and science objects available to all people to inspire them to invent and create, with the accent on commercial design and craftsmanship. Since it opened in 1857, its collection, now comprising over a million works, has become so encyclopaedic, it ranks as the world's largest decorative arts museum.

Bigger and bigger Its size is unmanageable: 11km (7 miles) of gallery space on six floors. Its

Clockwise from left: The V&A, which opened in 1857, now ranks as the world's largest museum of decorative arts; exhibits in the museum's The Renaissance City 1350–1600 display; the Jameel Gallery, where exhibits showcase Islamic art from the eighth and ninth centuries

content is even more so: barely five per cent of the 44,000 objects in the Indian department can be on show. Larger museum objects include whole London house facades, grand rooms and the Raphael Cartoons. Despite this, contemporary work has been energetically bought: more than 60 per cent of furniture entering the museum is 20th century.

Riches and rags Not every object in the museum is precious: there are everyday things, unique pieces and opportunities to discover a fascination for a new subject—perhaps lace, ironwork, tiles or Japanese textiles. See the lavishly refurbished British and Whiteley Silver galleries, the magnificent collections in the Medieval and Renaissance Galleries and the striking new Ceramics Gallery and Study Centre.

THE BASICS

www.vam.ac.uk

➕ C8

✉ Cromwell Road, SW7

☎ 020 7942 2000

🕐 Daily 10–5.45 (Fri 10–10)

🍴 Restaurant, café

🚇 South Kensington

♿ Very good

🎟 Free (except some special exhibitions)

❓ Free daily guided, introductory tours. Talks, courses, demonstrations, workshops and concerts

25 Westminster Abbey

HIGHLIGHTS

- Poet's Corner
- Sir Isaac Newton memorial
- Sir James Thornhill's window
- Henry VII's Chapel
- Edward the Confessor's Chapel
- St. Faith's Chapel
- Grave of the Unknown Soldier
- Little Cloister and College Garden
- Weekday sung evensong at 5pm

TIPS

- Attend a service and hear the choirboys, accompanied by the abbey organ.
- Free organ recitals, Sun 5.45; Summer organ festival (mid-Jul to mid-Aug).

The best time to be in the abbey is for the 8am service, sometimes held in St. Faith's Chapel. Follow this with a wander in the nave and cloisters before the crowds arrive.

The kernel of London's second city It was Edward the Confessor who in the 11th century began the rebuilding of the Benedictine abbey church of St. Peter, which was consecrated in 1065. The first sovereign to be crowned there was William the Conqueror, in 1066. Successive kings were patrons, as were the pilgrims who flocked to the Confessor's shrine. Henry III (1216–72) employed Master Henry de Reyns to begin the Gothic abbey that stands today, and Henry VII (1485–1509) built his Tudor chapel with its delicate fan vaulting. Since William I, all sovereigns have been crowned

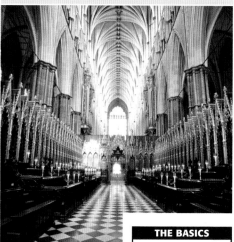

Clockwise from far left: The West Front; the Grave of the Unknown Soldier, adorned with Remembrance Day poppies; the shrine of Edward the Confessor, the abbey's founder; the choir stalls and ornate gilt altar; the abbey's magnificent vaulted ceiling

here—even after Henry VIII broke with Rome in 1533; and all were buried here up to George II (after which Windsor became the royal burial place, ▷ 79). It has also hosted 16 royal marriages, most recently that of Prince William and Catherine Middleton in 2011.

Daunting riches The abbey is massive, full of monuments and very popular. From the nave's west end enjoy the view of the abbey, then look over the Victorian Gothic choir screen into Henry V's chantry. Having explored the chapels, the royal necropolis and Poets' Corner, leave time for the quiet cloister with superb views of the flying buttresses supporting the nave. In the abbey museum you can see macabre wax effigies, including those of Queen Elizabeth I and Lord Nelson, and a 13th-century altarpiece.

THE BASICS

www.westminster-abbey.org

✚ J8

✉ Broad Sanctuary, SW1; entry by North Door

☎ 020 7222 5152

🕐 Abbey: Mon–Sat times vary, call or check website; no photography. Abbey Museum, College Garden: daily various hours. Closed before special services, Sun, 24–25 Dec, Good Fri and Commonwealth Day

🚇 Westminster, St. James's Park

🚆 Victoria

♿ Good

💷 Expensive

❓ Guided tours, audio guides

More to See

This section contains other great places to visit if you have more time. Some are in the heart of the city while others are a short journey away, found under Further Afield. This chapter also has fantastic excursions that you should set aside a whole day to visit.

MORE TO SEE

In the Heart of the City

30 ST. MARY AXE

This landmark tower, designed by Foster & Partners and affectionately known as 'The Gherkin', adds wit to the cluster of tall buildings in London's financial hub.

🚇 R4 ✉ 30 St. Mary Axe, EC3 🕐 Not open to the general public 🚇 Bank

ALBERT MEMORIAL

www.royalparks.org.uk

George Gilbert Scott's Gothic extravaganza dedicated to the creator of South Kensington, Prince Albert, celebrates Victorian achievement, with marble statues representing the Arts, Sciences, Industry and Continents. The finely carved frieze at its base depicts famous people in the Arts.

🚇 B7 ✉ Alexandra Gate, Kensington Gardens, SW7 🚇 South Kensington

ALL-HALLOWS-BY-THE-TOWER

www.allhallowsbythetower.org.uk

Founded in AD675, the church has a Saxon arch, a Roman pavement, a carving by Grinling Gibbons and the Crypt Museum.

🚇 R5 ✉ Byward Street, EC3 ☎ 020 7481 2928 🕐 Church: Mon–Fri 9–6, Sat–Sun 10–5. Closed public hols 🚇 Tower Hill 🎫 Free

APSLEY HOUSE (WELLINGTON MUSEUM)

www.english-heritage.org.uk

The splendid mansion was built for Arthur Wellesley, Duke of Wellington (1759–1852). The sumptuous interior houses his magnificent collection of paintings and decorative arts, with works by Velázquez and Rubens, as well as silver, porcelain and Canova's nude statue of Napoleon.

🚇 F7 ✉ Hyde Park Corner, W1 ☎ 020 7499 5676 🕐 Apr–Oct Wed–Sun 10–5; Nov–Mar 10–4 🚇 Hyde Park Corner 🎫 Moderate

BANK OF ENGLAND MUSEUM

www.bankofengland.co.uk/museum

Exhibits illustrate the history of Britain's monetary and banking system since 1694. Take time to appreciate the re-creations of Soane's rooms, and Sir Herbert Baker's Rotunda. The museum stages changing exhibitions.

The glittering Albert Memorial and nearby Albert Hall

30 St. Mary Axe, dubbed 'The Gherkin'

Q4 ⊠ Bartholomew Lane, EC2 ☎ 020
7601 5545 🕐 Mon–Fri 10–5 🚇 Bank
🎫 Free

BENJAMIN FRANKLIN HOUSE
www.benjaminfranklinhouse.org
The Founding Father of the United
States lived at this address for 15
years in the 18th century. His life
as an inventor and philosopher is
revealed through the innovative
Historical Experience shows.
K6 ⊠ 36 Craven Street, WC2 ☎ 020
7839 2006 🕐 Wed–Sun 12–5 🚇 Charing
Cross 🎫 Moderate

BOROUGH MARKET
www.boroughmarket.org.uk
Stallholders, many artisan produc-
ers, sell their goods at London's
most exciting food market.
Q6 ⊠ Southwark Street, SE1 🕐 Thu
11–5, Fri 12–4, Sat 8–5 🚊 London Bridge
🚇 London Bridge

BRITISH LIBRARY
www.bl.uk
Colin St. John Wilson's 1998 red-
brick building houses the nation's
books and manuscripts, with

public galleries and a piazza.
Changing exhibitions showcase
different aspects of the library's
collection.
J1 ⊠ 96 Euston Road, NW1 ☎ 0843
208 1144 🕐 Mon–Fri 9.30–6, Tue 9.30–8,
Sat 9.30–5, Sun 11–5 🍴 Café, restaurant
🚇 Kings Cross 🎫 Donation

BROMPTON ORATORY
www.bromptonoratory.com
Standing next door to the V&A, the
flamboyant Oratory of St. Philip
Neri was built in 1876 and given a
sumptuous, sculpture-filled interior.
C8 ⊠ Brompton Road, SW7 ☎ 020
7808 0900 🕐 Daily 6.30am–8pm
🚇 South Kensington 🎫 Donation

CHARLES DICKENS MUSEUM
www.dickensmuseum.com
Visit the house where Dickens
wrote novels *Nicholas Nickleby*
and *Oliver Twist*. A £3.1 million
restoration project is due for completion in 2012, the bicentenary of
Dickens's birth.
L2 ⊠ 48 Doughty Street, WC1 ☎ 020
7405 2127 🕐 Daily 10–5 🚇 Russell
Square 🎫 Moderate

Fresh shellfish at Borough Market

*The British Library piazza, with
Eduardo Paolozzi's bronze statue*

CHRISTCHURCH SPITALFIELDS

www.christchurchspitalfields.org

Nicholas Hawksmoor's 1750 masterpiece has been finely restored and is often used for concerts.

🚇 S3 ✉ Fournier Street, E1 ☎ 020 7377 6793 🕐 Tue 11–4, Sun 1–4 🚉 Liverpool Street 💷 Donation

CHURCHILL WAR ROOMS

www.iwm.org.uk

Churchill directed Britain's war effort from these secret rooms, evocatively kept as they were in 1945. Exhibits in the Churchill Museum tell of his life and times.

🚇 J7 ✉ Clive Steps, King Charles Street, SW1 ☎ 020 7930 6961 🕐 Daily 9.30–6 🚉 St. James's Park, Westminster 💷 Expensive

CITY HALL

www.london.gov.uk

Architect Sir Norman Foster's distinctive glass building is home to the Mayor of London and the Greater London Authority.

🚇 R6 ✉ The Queen's Walk, SE1 ☎ 020 7983 4000 🕐 Mon–Thu 8.30–6, Fri 8.30–5.30 🚉 London Bridge 💷 Free

CLARENCE HOUSE

www.royal.gov.uk

Built for Prince William, Duke of Clarence and later William IV, this was the late Queen Mother's London home, now renovated by its current resident, the Prince of Wales. Five rooms used by Prince Charles and the Duchess of Cornwall for official engagements can be seen. All tickets are timed and must be prebooked.

🚇 H7 ✉ Off the Mall, SW1 ☎ 020 7766 7303 🕐 Aug Mon–Fri 10–4, Sat–Sun 10–5.30 🚉 St. James's Park, Green Park 💷 Moderate

CLEOPATRA'S NEEDLE

The 26m (86ft) pink granite obelisk was made in Egypt in 1450BC and records the triumphs of Rameses the Great.

🚇 K6 ✉ Victoria Embankment, WC2 🚉 Embankment, Charing Cross 💷 Free

CLOCKMAKERS' MUSEUM

www.clockmakers.org

This collection of exquisite timepieces tick-tocking away includes Thomas Tompion masterpieces.

City Hall, home to the Greater London Authority

➕ P4 ✉ Guildhall Library, Aldermanbury, EC2 ☎ 020 7332 1868 🕐 Mon–Sat 9.30–4.45 🚇 St. Paul's, Bank 🎫 Free

COVENT GARDEN PIAZZA

London's first square was laid out in the 1630s by architect Inigo Jones. It later became a fruit and vegetable market. Redeveloped in the 1980s, the piazza and market quickly became a popular meeting place, mixing quirky shops with lively street entertainment.
➕ K5 🚇 Covent Garden

DESIGN MUSEUM

www.designmuseum.org
Founded by design guru Sir Terence Conran, the museum hosts temporary exhibitions, covering all aspects of modern design.
➕ S7 ✉ 28 Shad Thames, SE1 ☎ 0870 833 9955 🕐 Daily 10–5.45 🍴 Café, restaurant 🚇 Tower Hill, London Bridge 🚉 London Bridge 🎫 Moderate

DR. JOHNSON'S HOUSE

www.drjohnsonshouse.org
Dr. Samuel Johnson lived here between 1748 and 1759 while compiling his dictionary. Inside, the house has panelled rooms, period furniture, prints and portraits.
➕ M4 ✉ 17 Gough Square, EC4 ☎ 020 7353 3745 🕐 May–Sep Mon–Sat 11–5.30; Oct–Apr Mon–Sat 11–5 🚇 Chancery Lane, Temple, Holborn 🚉 Blackfriars 🎫 Inexpensive

EROS

Alfred Gilbert's memorial (1893) to the philanthropic 7th Earl of Shaftesbury (1801–85), *The Angel of Christian Charity*, is popularly referred to as Eros, although it actually depicts Anteros, the god of selfless love.
➕ H5 ✉ Piccadilly Circus, W1 🚇 Piccadilly Circus

FOUNDLING MUSEUM

www.foundlingmuseum.org.uk
When Thomas Coran founded a hospice for abandoned children in 1739, Handel and Hogarth helped raise funds. Both the building and the art are magnificent.
➕ K2 ✉ 40 Brunswick Square, WC1 ☎ 020 7841 3600 🕐 Tue–Sat 10–5, Sun 12–5 🚇 Russell Square 🎫 Moderate

A street performer entertains the crowds at Covent Garden Piazza

Eros, at the heart of Piccadilly Circus

GOLDEN HINDE

www.goldenhinde.com

The ship is an exact replica of the 16th-century galleon in which Sir Francis Drake circumnavigated the globe.

➕ Q6 ✉ St. Mary Overie Dock, Cathedral Street, SE1 ☎ 0870 011 8700 🕐 Usually daily 10 until dusk, but hours vary 🚇 London Bridge 🚉 London Bridge 💰 Moderate

GREEN PARK

www.royalparks.gov.uk

Covering 19ha (47 acres), Green Park is famous for its mature trees, tree-lined avenues and spring daffodils.

➕ G7 ✉ SW1 ☎ 0300 061 2000 🕐 Daily dawn–dusk 🚇 Green Park, Hyde Park Corner 💰 Free

GUILDHALL ART GALLERY

www.guildhall-art-gallery.org.uk

The gallery offers two remarkable things to see: the Guildhall's quirky collection of mostly British pictures, and part of Roman London's huge amphitheatre, built in AD200 and rediscovered in 1988.

➕ P4 ✉ Guildhall Yard, Gresham Street, EC2 ☎ 020 7332 3700 🕐 Mon–Sat 10–5, Sun 12–4 🚇 St. Paul's, Bank 💰 Free

HANDEL HOUSE MUSEUM

www.handelhouse.org

Anyone who plays a musical instrument or sings *The Messiah* should visit the composer's London home from 1723 until 1759. The museum hosts weekly concerts and other musical events.

➕ G5 ✉ 25 Brook Street, W1 ☎ 020 7495 1685 🕐 Tue–Wed, Fri–Sat 10–6, Thu 10–8, Sun 12–6 🚇 Bond Street 💰 Moderate

HAYWARD GALLERY

www.southbankcentre.co.uk

Major contemporary art exhibitions are staged in a stark 1960s setting.

➕ L6 ✉ Belvedere Road, SE1 ☎ 0844 875 0070 🕐 Daily 10–6 during exhibitions 🚇 Waterloo 🚉 Waterloo 💰 Moderate–expensive; some exhibitions free

HMS BELFAST

www.iwm.org.uk

Clamber up, down and around this 1938 war cruiser, visiting the

The retired 1938 war cruiser HMS Belfast

cabins, gun turrets, dining hall, bridge and boiler-room.

🔲 R6 ✉ Morgan's Lane, Tooley Street, SE1
☎ 020 7940 6300 🕐 Mar–Oct daily 10–6;
Nov–Feb 10–5 🍴 Café 🚇 London Bridge
🚇 London Bridge 💷 Expensive; children
under 16 free

HOLY TRINITY, SLOANE SQUARE
www.holytrinitysloanesquare.co.uk
London's best Arts and Crafts
church, designed by J.D. Sedding,
has glass by Burne-Jones, William
Morris and others. Note the huge
east window with 48 panels
depicting saints.

🔲 E9 ✉ Sloane Square, SW1 ☎ 020
7730 7270 🕐 Mon–Sat 8.30–5.30, Sun
8.30–1.30 🚇 Sloane Square 💷 Donation

HUNTERIAN MUSEUM
www.rcseng.ac.uk
See the brilliantly ghoulish exhibits,
with 3,500 specimens, from the
anatomical collection of John
Hunter.

🔲 L4 ✉ Royal College of Surgeons,
Lincoln's Inn Fields, WC2 ☎ 020 7869 6560
🕐 Tue–Sat 10–5 🚇 Holborn 💷 Free

HYDE PARK
www.royalparks.gov.uk
One of London's largest open
spaces, the park was tamed in the
18th century. Don't miss the views
from the Serpentine Bridge, the
Rose Garden or the Diana, Princess
of Wales Memorial Fountain.

🔲 E6 ✉ W2 ☎ 0300 061 2000 🕐 Daily
5am–midnight 🍴 Restaurant, café
🚇 Marble Arch, High Street Kensington,
Hyde Park Corner 💷 Free

IMPERIAL WAR MUSEUM
www.iwm.org.uk
The museum focuses on the social
impact of 20th-century warfare
through film, painting and sound
archives. The Holocaust Museum
is not suitable for children.

🔲 M8 ✉ Lambeth Road, SE1 ☎ 020
7416 5000 🕐 Daily 10–6 🍴 Café
🚇 Lambeth North, Elephant & Castle,
Waterloo 🚇 Waterloo 💷 Free

LONDON TRANSPORT MUSEUM
www.ltmuseum.co.uk
High-tech exhibits explore
London's communities, and the

The Diana, Princess of Wales Memorial Fountain, Hyde Park

past and future of the capital's transport system.

🚇 K5 ✉ Covent Garden Piazza, WC2 ☎ 020 7379 6344 🕐 Sat–Thu 10–6, Fri 11–6 🍴 Café 🚇 Covent Garden 🚉 Charing Cross 💷 Moderate

MADAME TUSSAUD'S

www.madame-tussauds.com/London
See how many famous people you can identify, from Shakespeare to Madonna.

🚇 E3 ✉ Marylebone Road, NW1 ☎ 0871 894 3000 🕐 Daily 9.30–5.30 🍴 Café 🚇 Baker Street 💷 Expensive; family ticket

PETER PAN STATUE

George Frampton's statue (1912) commemorating J.M. Barrie's fictional creation, the boy who never grew up, stands in Kensington Gardens.

🚇 B6 ✉ Long Water, Kensington Gardens 🚇 Lancaster Gate

PETRIE MUSEUM

www.ucl.ac.uk
The ancient spoils of many Egyptologists' explorations are on display at the hard-to-find Petrie Museum (it's close to the rear of the British Museum). With 80,000 objects, it's one of the world's greatest collections of Egyptian and Sudanese archaeology.

🚇 J2 ✉ Univeristy College London, Malet Place, WC1E ☎ 020 7679 2884 🕐 Tue–Sat 1–5 🚇 Euston Square 💷 Free

PHOTOGRAPHERS' GALLERY

www.photonet.org.uk
An £8.7-million project completed in 2011 has transformed an Edwardian warehouse into a state-of-the-art home for the Photographers' Gallery. The gallery has three floors of exhibition space, a bookshop and a café, and hosts talks and events.

🚇 H4 ✉ 16–18 Ramillies Street, W1 ☎ 0845 262 1618 🕐 Tue–Fri 11–8, Sat 11–6, Sun 12–6 🚇 Oxford Circus 💷 Free

REGENT'S PARK AND ZSL LONDON ZOO

www.royalparks.gov.uk; www.zsl.org
Regent's Park has vast rose gardens, a boating lake, sports facilities and an open-air theatre in the summer. London Zoo, in its

The London Transport Museum celebrates the capital's transport system

Wax figures at Madame Tussaud's

northeastern corner, is popular
with children and offers activities
during holidays.
➕ Off map at D1–F1 ✉ Outer Circle,
Regent's Park NW1 ☎ Park: 0300 061 2000.
Zoo: 020 7722 3333 🕐 Park: daily 5am–
dusk. Zoo: mid-Jul to Aug daily 10–6; Mar to
mid-Jul, Sep–Oct 10–5.30; Nov–Feb 10–4
🍴 Cafés 🚇 Regent's Park, Camden Town
💷 Park: free. Zoo: expensive

ROYAL ACADEMY OF ARTS
www.royalacademy.org.uk
The Royal Academy hosts major
art shows, plus the annual
Summer Exhibition, held every
year since 1769. Don't miss the
rooftop Sackler Galleries.
➕ H5 ✉ Burlington House, Piccadilly, W1
☎ 020 7300 8000 🕐 Sat–Thu 10–6, Fri
10–10 🍴 Restaurant, café 🚇 Green Park,
Piccadilly 💷 Expensive

ST. BARTHOLOMEW-THE-
GREAT
www.greatstbarts.com
Built in 1123, this is the City's only
12th-century monastic church, and
its best surviving piece of large-
scale Romanesque architecture.

➕ N3 ✉ West Smithfield, EC1 ☎ 020
7606 5171 🕐 Mon–Fri 8.30–5 (4pm mid-
Nov to mid--Feb), Sat 8.30–4, Sun 8.30–8.
Sun services at 9, 11, 6.30 🚇 Barbican,
Farringdon, St. Paul's 🚉 Farringdon
♿ Good 💷 Inexpensive

ST. JAMES'S, PICCADILLY
www.st-james-piccadilly.org
Wren's church (1682–84), built
for the local aristocracy, has a
sumptuous interior. Some superb
concerts are held here.
➕ H6 ✉ 197 Piccadilly, W1 ☎ 020 7734
4511 🕐 Daily 8–6.30 🍴 Café
🚇 Piccadilly Circus 💷 Donation

ST. KATHARINE DOCKS
www.skdocks.co.uk
Luxury yachts now fill the marina
close to Tower Bridge and the
Tower of London where valuable
cargoes were once landed, and
restaurants, bars, shops and
apartments fill the former
warehouses.
➕ S6 ✉ St. Katharine's Way, E1 ☎ 020
7488 0555 🚇 Tower Hill 🚉 Tower
Gateway (DLR), Fenchurch Street 🚢 Tower
Pier, St. Katharine's Pier 💷 Free

The Royal Academy of Arts

*A titi monkey, one of the
inhabitants of ZSL London Zoo*

ST. MARGARET, LOTHBURY

www.stml.org.uk

Wren's church (1692) retains its huge carved screen with soaring eagle and carved pulpit tester. It offers a weekday ministry for the City of London.

➕ Q4 ✉ Lothbury, EC2 ☎ 020 7726 4878 🕓 Mon–Fri 7.15–5.15 🚇 Bank ✋ Donation

SEA LIFE LONDON AQUARIUM

www.visitsealife.com/london

More than 3,000 forms of marine life fill this aquatic spectacular.

➕ L7 ✉ County Hall, SE1 ☎ 0871 663 1678 🕓 Mon–Thu 10–6, Fri–Sun 10–7 🚇 Westminster ✋ Expensive

SOUTHWARK CATHEDRAL

http://cathedral.southwark.anglican.org

The fine stone building is powerfully atmospheric of its medieval origins, despite much rebuilding. Inside, there is a fine choir and some interesting monuments.

➕ Q6 ✉ London Bridge, SE1 ☎ 020 7367 6700 🕓 Mon–Fri 8–6, Sat–Sun 8.30–6 🍴 Cafe 🚇 London Bridge 🚉 London Bridge ✋ Donation

SPENCER HOUSE

www.spencerhouse.co.uk

A lavishly restored Palladian mansion, Spencer House is a rare survivor of 18th-century aristocratic St. James's and Mayfair. Eight rooms with gilded decorations, period paintings and furniture are open to the public, along with the authentically restored garden.

➕ H6 ✉ 27 St. James's Place, SW1 ☎ 020 7499 8620 🕓 Sun 10.30–5.45. Closed Jan and Aug. Booking advised, compulsory guided tour 🚇 Green Park ✋ Moderate; no children under 10

TEMPLE CHURCH

www.templechurch.com

Begun about 1160, this private chapel built by the Knights Templar to a circular plan stands at the heart of the Inns of Court. You can visit the Temple gardens and the 16th-century Middle Temple Hall. The church hosts fine music and organ recitals; check the website for details.

➕ M4 ✉ Temple, EC4 ☎ 020 7353 3470 🕓 Opening times vary, check website. Sun services 🚇 Temple ✋ Donation

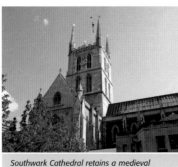

Southwark Cathedral retains a medieval appearance despite much rebuilding

Temple Church in the Inns of Court

TEMPLE OF MITHRAS

Right on the open street, the Roman temple foundations of AD240–250 testify to the cult of the Persian god Mithras.

➕ P5 ✉ Temple Court, Queen Victoria Street, EC4 🚇 Mansion House, Bank

TRAFALGAR SQUARE

Sir Edwin Landseer's lions protect Nelson's Column, erected to commemorate the 1805 Battle of Trafalgar, at the heart of London's most iconic square. The fountains were added in 1845. Bronze statues stand on three of the plinths, while the fourth is used to exhibit changing works by contemporary artists.

➕ J6 🍴 Restaurants and cafés 🚇 Charing Cross 🚉 Charing Cross 🎟 Free

VINOPOLIS

www.vinopolis.co.uk

The warren of rooms at Vinopolis is devoted to the world's wine-growing regions, with films, experts, tastings and a restaurant.

➕ P6 ✉ 1 Bank End, SE1 ☎ 020 7940 3000 🕐 Thu–Sat 12–10, Sun 12–6; last entry 2.5 hours before closing. Prebooking essential 🚇 London Bridge 🚉 London Bridge 🎟 Expensive, includes audio guide and tastings

WALLACE COLLECTION

www.wallacecollection.org

Old Masters, French 18th-century paintings, furniture and porcelain, and a world-class armoury are all housed in this historic London town house, with a good restaurant in the courtyard.

➕ F4 ✉ Hertford House, Manchester Square, W1 ☎ 020 7563 9500 🕐 Daily 10–5 🍴 Restaurant, café 🚇 Marble Arch, Bond Street 🎟 Free

WINSTON CHURCHILL'S BRITAIN AT WAR EXPERIENCE

www.britainatwar.co.uk

The collection pays tribute to ordinary people who lived their lives against the backdrop of air raids, the blackout, rationing and evacuation in World War II.

➕ R6 ✉ 64–66 Tooley Street, SE1 ☎ 020 7403 3171 🕐 Apr–Oct daily 10–5; Nov–Mar 10–4.30 🚇 London Bridge 🚉 London Bridge 🎟 Expensive

Bustling Trafalgar Square, a popular meeting place

Further Afield

CANARY WHARF

www.canarywharf.com

César Pelli's soaring, pyramid-topped tower (1991) dominates a premier business district.

➕ Off map at S5 ✉ 1 Canada Square, Canary Wharf, E14 🕐 Public spaces are open, not buildings 🚇 Canary Wharf

CHELSEA PHYSIC GARDEN

www.chelseaphysicgarden.co.uk

This 17th-century walled garden was laid out by Sir Hans Sloane for the Society of Apothecaries.

➕ Off map at C9 ✉ 66 Royal Hospital Road, SW3 ☎ 020 7349 6458 🕐 Apr–Oct Tue–Fri 12–5, Sun 2–6 🍴 Café 🚇 Sloane Square 💷 Moderate

CHISWICK HOUSE

www.chgt.org.uk

Lord Burlington's exquisite country villa (1725–29) has superb formal gardens and conservatories.

➕ Off map at A9 ✉ Burlington Lane, W4 ☎ 020 8995 0508 🕐 House: Apr daily 10–5; May–Oct Sun–Wed 10–5; Nov–Dec pre-booked tours only. Garden: daily 7–dusk 🍴 Café 🚇 Turnham Green 🚆 Chiswick 💷 House: moderate. Garden: free

DULWICH PICTURE GALLERY

www.dulwichpicturegallery.org.uk

Opened in 1814, this was England's first public art gallery.

➕ Off map at N9 ✉ Gallery Road, SE21 ☎ 020 8693 5254 🕐 Tue–Fri 10–5, Sat–Sun 11–5 🍴 Café 🚆 North or West Dulwich 💷 Moderate

FIREPOWER MUSEUM

www.firepower.org.uk

Exhibits here range from Roman trebuchets to an Iraqi supergun, with plenty of visitor participation.

➕ Off map at S7 ✉ The Royal Arsenal, Woolwich, SE18 ☎ 020 8855 7755 🕐 Wed–Sun 10.30–5; school hols daily 🍴 Café 🚆 Woolwich Arsenal 🚢 Ferry from Greenwich 💷 Moderate

HAM HOUSE

www.nationaltrust.org.uk

The house and garden at this Thameside baroque mansion have been meticulously restored.

➕ Off map at A10 ✉ Ham, Richmond, Surrey ☎ 020 8940 1950 🕐 House: Mar–Oct Sat–Thu 12–4. Gardens: all year daily 11–5 🍴 Tearoom 🚆 Richmond, then bus 371 💷 Expensive

Historic Ham House and gardens, built in 1610 on the banks of the Thames

The Museum of London Docklands

HAMPSTEAD HEATH
www.cityoflondon.gov.uk
Hampstead Heath offers 325ha (800 acres) of open countryside to enjoy in north London.
➕ Off map at H1 ✉ 8km (5 miles) NW of Trafalgar Square ☎ 020 7482 7073 for visitor information ⏰ Daily 8am–dusk
🚇 Hampstead 🎫 Free

JEWISH MUSEUM
www.jewishmuseum.org.uk
The museum's exhibitions and activities explore Jewish history, culture and heritage.
➕ Off map at J1 ✉ 129–131 Albert Street, NW1 ☎ 020 7284 7384 ⏰ Sun–Thu 10–5, Fri 10–2 🍴 Kosher café 🚇 Camden Town 🎫 Moderate

KENWOOD HOUSE
www.english-heritage.org.uk
Restyled by Robert Adam, this country house lies outside pretty Hampstead village. Its walls are hung with Rembrandts, Romneys, Vermeers and Gainsboroughs and its landscaped parkland provides grand views. In summer, evening concerts are held in the grounds.

The V&A Museum of Childhood

➕ Off map at H1 ✉ Hampstead Lane, NW3 ☎ 020 8348 1286 ⏰ Daily 11.30–4 🍴 Café 🚇 Hampstead Heath 🎫 Free

LONDON WETLAND CENTRE
www.wwt.org.uk
The Wildfowl and Wetlands Trust administers 42ha (104 acres) of lakes, ponds, grassland and mud-flats that attract a variety of wildlife.
➕ Off map at A9 ✉ Queen Elizabeth's Walk, SW13 ☎ 020 8409 4400 ⏰ Mar–Oct daily 9.30–6; Nov–Feb 9.30–5 🍴 Café 🚇 Hammersmith, then bus 283 🚉 Barnes, then bus 33, 72 🎫 Expensive

MUSEUM OF LONDON DOCKLANDS
www.museumoflondon.org.uk/docklands
The museum tells the story of London's river, port and people from Roman times until now. It also hosts events and tours.
➕ Off map at S5 ✉ No. 1 Warehouses, West India Quay, Canary Wharf, E14 ☎ 020 7001 9844 ⏰ Daily 10–6 🍴 Restaurant 🚇 West India Quay, Canary Wharf 🎫 Free

V&A MUSEUM OF CHILDHOOD
www.vam.ac.uk/moc
Exhibits here explore playtime from 1600 to the present day, with Noah's arks, dolls, toy soldiers and even a model circus.
➕ Off map at S2 ✉ Cambridge Heath Road, E2 ☎ 020 8983 5200/2415 ⏰ Daily 10–5.45 🍴 Café 🚇 Bethnal Green 🚉 Bethnal Green 🎫 Free

WHITECHAPEL ART GALLERY
www.whitechapelgallery.org
The gallery is the hub of the East End contemporary art activities.
➕ S4 ✉ 80 Whitechapel High Street, E1 ☎ 020 7522 7888 ⏰ Tue–Wed, Fri–Sun 11–6, Thu 11–9 🍴 Café 🚇 Aldgate East 🎫 Free

Excursions

HAMPTON COURT PALACE

www.hrp.org.uk

This is London's most impressive royal palace, well worth the 35-minute train journey out from central London.

When King Henry VIII dismissed Cardinal Wolsey in 1529, he took over his already ostentatious Tudor palace and enlarged it. Successive monarchs altered and repaired both the palace and its 12ha (29 acres) of Tudor and baroque gardens.

The best way to visit this huge collection of chambers, courtyards and state apartments is to follow one of the six clearly indicated routes—perhaps Henry VIII's State Apartments or the King's Apartments built for William III, immaculately restored after a devastating fire. Highlights include Henry VIII's Great Hall, which is recognized as England's finest medieval hall. William Shakespeare performed plays here between 1603 and 1604. The Chapel Royal, still in use after 450 years, should not to be missed. Neither should the vast Tudor kitchens, built to feed Henry VIII's court, providing over 600 meals twice a day. Live cookery demonstrations are given every month; check the website for dates of these and other events.

You can easily spend a day at the palace, but allow at least three hours for your visit. Do not miss the formal Tudor gardens that reach down to the River Thames, the famous Maze and restored Privy Garden, looking now as it would have done when it was created for William III in 1702.

Children love Hampton Court, not least because there are so many events and activities designed especially for them, including costumed presentations and family audio guides and trails.

Distance: 16km (10 miles)
Journey Time: 35 min
✉ East Molesey, Surrey ☎ 0844 482 7777
🕐 Apr–Oct daily 10–6; Nov–Mar 10–4.30
🍴 Café, restaurant 💷 Expensive
🚆 Waterloo to Hampton Court
🚢 Riverboat to Hampton Court

The beautiful formal flower gardens at Hampton Court Palace

The palace's courtyard and entrance gate

WINDSOR

www.windsor.gov.uk
www.royalcollection.org.uk

Fairy-tale towers and turrets make this the ultimate royal castle. An official residence of Her Majesty the Queen, it's the oldest and largest occupied castle in the world. As it is a working royal palace, opening times can change, so it's best to phone or check the website for the latest information.

Begun by William the Conqueror and rebuilt in stone by Henry II, the castle has been embellished over the centuries. The richly decorated State Apartments are hung with paintings by Old Masters. The tombs of 10 sovereigns, including Henry VIII and Charles I, lie amid the fine Gothic architecture of St. George's Chapel, setting for the service of dedication following the marriage of Prince Charles and the Duchess of Cornwall in 2005.

Should the State Apartments or Chapel be closed, there is still much to see. The Drawings Gallery has changing exhibitions, and don't miss Queen Mary's Dolls' House,

designed by Edward Lutyens. Some 1,500 craftspeople were involved in its construction.

Changing the Guard takes place at 11am daily, April to end July, and on alternate days for the rest of the year, weather permitting, but never on a Sunday.

Outside the castle lie Windsor's pretty, medieval cobblestoned lanes, Christopher Wren's Guildhall and the delightful Theatre Royal. Beyond it, you can explore 1,950ha (4,700-acre) Windsor Great Park and cross the river footbridge to Eton, a heritage town famed for its public school.

Distance: 37km (23 miles)
Journey Time: 40–55 min
🛈 Windsor Royal Shopping, Thames Street
☎ 01753 743900 🕐 May–Aug Mon–Fri 9.30–5.30, Sat 9.30–5, Sun 10–4; Sep–Apr Mon–Sat 10–5, Sun 10–4 🚉 Waterloo to Windsor & Eton Riverside, Paddington to Windsor & Eton Central
Windsor Castle
☎ 01753 831118 🕐 Mar–Oct daily 9.45–5.15; Nov–Feb 9.45–4.15
💷 Expensive

Stately Windsor Castle

Great Park and the Long Walk entrance to Windsor Castle

City Tours

This section contains self-guided tours that will help you explore the sights in each of the city's regions. Each tour is designed to take a day, with a map pinpointing the recommended places along the way. There is a quick reference guide at the end of each tour, listing everything you need in that region, so you know exactly what's close by.

CITY TOURS

South Bank

With mesmerizing river views, exciting contemporary art at Tate Modern, medieval history at Southwark Cathedral, world-class concert halls and a theatrical tradition dating back to Shakespeare's time, the South Bank has plenty to entice visitors.

Morning
Start at **Tower Bridge** and set the scene for your day with high-level, panoramic views of London and the River Thames. Then stroll among the converted warehouses of Shad Thames, home to the **Design Museum** (▷ 69) and numerous shops and cafés. Join the well-signed riverside Thames Path, passing the distinctive **City Hall** (▷ 68), seat of government, and the moored war cruiser **HMS *Belfast*** (right, ▷ 70).

Mid-morning
From Tooley Street, zigzag under **London Bridge** to visit **Southwark Cathedral** (left, ▷ 74). Admire the soaring nave, choir and 16th-century Great Screen, and look for stained-glass windows depicting famous Southwark inhabitants, including Chaucer and Shakespeare. The **Harvard Chapel** reveals some of the cathedral's many links with America.

Lunch
Borough Market (right, ▷ 67) is nearby and the perfect location for lunch, especially on Thursdays to Saturdays when it is packed with enticing food stalls and the restaurants are particularly lively.

Afternoon

Return to the riverside, passing the fine 14th-century rose window in the ruins of **Winchester Palace**, to see the replica of Sir Francis Drake's galleon, *Golden Hinde* (right, ▷ 70). Walk through medieval, cobblestoned Clink Street, once the site of a notorious prison. Passing under Southwark Bridge, restaurants, cafés and pubs with river views line the route to **Shakespeare's Globe** (▷ 139), a faithful reconstruction of an Elizabethan open-air theatre. The excellent guided tour of the theatre is not to be missed.

Mid-afternoon

Explore the contemporary art at **Tate Modern** (▷ 54–55) and take time for tea in its café with a view. Continue your stroll along the Thames Path, enjoying views of the architecture lining the opposite bank of the river. Have a look in the crafts studios on the lower floors of the **Oxo Tower** (left) and in nearby **Gabriel's Wharf**, before you reach **Waterloo Bridge**—you may find a second-hand books market under its arches—and the **South Bank** arts complex.

Dinner

There's a vast choice of restaurants around here, but if you're up for somewhere smart with unmatched views, book a table at the **Oxo Tower Bar, Brasserie and Restaurant** (▷ 149).

Evening

With concerts by world-class musicians at the **Royal Festival Hall** (▷ 138), plays at the **National Theatre** (▷ 136) and films at **BFI Southbank** (▷ 133), you're spoiled for choice for entertainment in this part of London. Free live music events are often held in the early evening. Alternatively, a ride on the **London Eye** (▷ 28) at night is a magical experience.

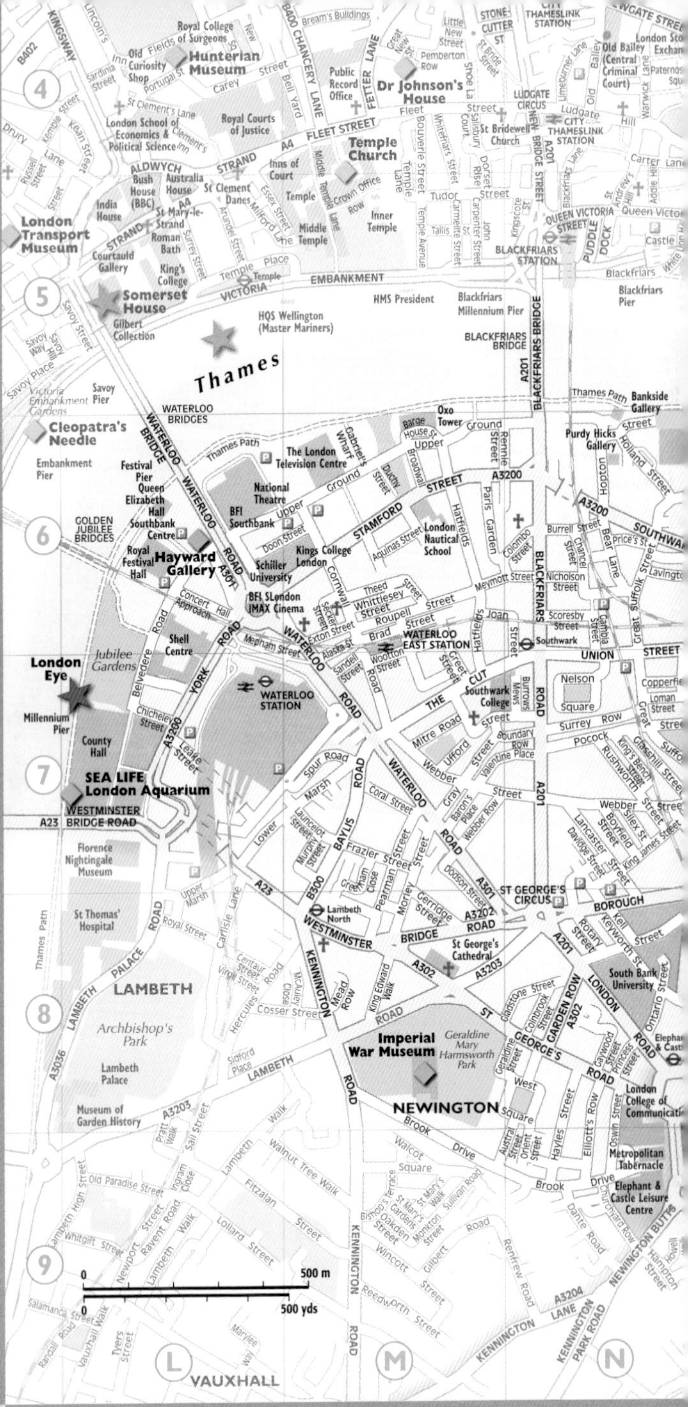

Royal College of Surgeons
Hunterian Museum
Old Curiosity Shop
Lincoln's Inn Fields
Kingsway
B402
Portugal St
Carey Street
Bell Yard
B400 Chancery Lane
Fetter Lane
Public Record Office
Dr Johnson's House
Pemberton Row
Bream's Buildings
Little New Street
Great New St
Shoe La
St Bride Street
Stonecutter St
City Thameslink Station
Old Bailey (Central Criminal Court)
London Stock Exchange
Paternoster Sq
Newgate Street
Ludgate Circus
Ludgate Hill
Limeburner Lane
St Clement's Lane
London School of Economics & Political Science
Clement's Inn
Royal Courts of Justice
Fleet Street
A4
Temple Church
Bouverie Street
Whitefriars Street
Salisbury Court
St Bridewell Church
New Bridge Street
A201
City Thameslink Station
Carter Lane
Blackfriars Lane
Drury Lane
Kemble Street
Kean Street
Russell Street
Aldwych
Bush House (BBC)
Australia House
India House
Strand
St Clement Danes
Inns of Court
Temple
Middle Temple Lane
Crown Office Row
Inner Temple
Temple Lane
Tudor Street
Dorset Rise
Carpenter Street
Carmelite Street
Tallis St
John Street
Temple Avenue
Kingscote St
Queen Victoria Street
Puddle Dock
Castle
Blackfriars Station
London Transport Museum
St Mary-le-Strand
Roman Bath
Surrey Street
Arundel Street
Essex Street
Milford Lane
Middle Temple
Courtauld Gallery
King's College
Temple Place
Temple
Victoria Embankment
Somerset House
Gilbert Collection
Savoy Street
Savoy Hill
Savoy Way
Savoy Place
HMS President
HQS Wellington (Master Mariners)
Blackfriars Millennium Pier
Blackfriars Bridge
Blackfriars
Blackfriars Pier
Thames
Victoria Embankment Gardens
Savoy Pier
Waterloo Bridges
Waterloo Bridge
Cleopatra's Needle
Embankment Pier
Thames Path
Bankside Gallery
Oxo Tower
Barge House St
Gabriel's Wharf
Upper Ground
Rennie Street
Purdy Hicks Gallery
Holland Street
Hopton Street
The London Television Centre
National Theatre
Duchy Street
Broadwall
Stamford Street
A3200
Festival Pier
Queen Elizabeth Hall
Southbank Centre
BFI Southbank
Hatfields
Paris Garden
Burrell Street
Chancel Street
Bear Lane
Price's St
Southwark Street
Golden Jubilee Bridges
Royal Festival Hall
Hayward Gallery
A301
Waterloo Road
Doon Street
Schiller University
Kings College London
Aquinas Street
London Nautical School
Colombo Street
Blackfriars Road
Nicholson Street
Great Suffolk Street
Lavington St
Concert Hall Approach
BFI London IMAX Cinema
Cornwall Road
Theed Street
Whittlesey Street
Roupell Street
Meymott Street
Scoresby Street
Gambia Street
Shell Centre
Belvedere Road
York Road
Sekford Street
Exton Street
Mepham Street
Waterloo
Alaska St
Brad Street
Waterloo East Station
Joan Street
Southwark
Union Street
London Eye
Jubilee Gardens
Waterloo Station
Sandell Street
Wootton Street
Greet Street
The Cut
Southwark College
Burrows Mews
Nelson Square
Copperfield St
Loman Street
Millennium Pier
Chicheley Street
County Hall
A3200
Leake Street
Mitre Road
Ufford Street
Boundary Row
Valentine Place
Surrey Row
Pocock Street
Glasshill Street
King's Bench Street
Rushworth Street
Spur Road
Marsh
Baylis Road
Coral Street
Webber Street
SEA LIFE London Aquarium
Westminster Bridge Road
A23
Lower Marsh
Launcelot Street
Murphy Street
Frazier Street
Gray Street
Baron's Place
Webber Row
Boyfield Street
Silex St
Lancaster Street
Davidge Street
King James Street
Florence Nightingale Museum
Greenham Close
Pearman Street
Morley Street
Dodson Street
St George's Circus
Borough Road
Upper Marsh
B300
Lambeth North
Gerridge Street
A3202
Rotary Street
Keyworth St
Kell Street
St Thomas' Hospital
Royal Street
Carlisle Lane
Westminster Bridge Road
Thames Path
Centaur Street
Virgil Street
McAuley Close
Kennington Road
Mead Row
King Edward Walk
St George's Cathedral
A302
A3203
South Bank University
Ontario Street
Lambeth Palace Road
Lambeth
Hercules Road
Cosser Street
St George's Road
Gladstone Street
Colnbrook Street
Garden Row
London Road
Elephant & Castle
Archbishop's Park
A3036
Lambeth Palace
Sidford Place
Lambeth Road
Imperial War Museum
Geraldine Mary Harmsworth Park
Geraldine Street
Gaywood Street
Princess Street
West Square
London College of Communication
Museum of Garden History
A3203
Pratt Walk
Newington
Brook Drive
Austral Street
Orient Street
Hayles Street
Elliott's Row
Oswin Street
Metropolitan Tabernacle
Walk
Walcot Square
Sullivan Road
Lambeth Walk
Walnut Tree Walk
Old Paradise Street
Ingram Close
Fitzalan Street
Bishop's Terrace
St Mary's Gardens
St Mary's Walk
Oakden Street
Monkton Street
Elephant & Castle Leisure Centre
Churchyard Row
Dante Road
Newington Butts
Lambeth High Street
Newport Street
Ravent Road
Lollard Street
Wincott Street
Gilbert Road
Renfrew Road
Howell Walk
Hampton Street
Whitgift Street
500 m
500 yds
Reedworth Street
A3204
Kennington Lane
Kennington Park Road
Salamanca Street
Randall Road
Vauxhall Walk
Tyers Street
Marylee Way
Vauxhall
4
5
6
7
8
9
L
M
N

CITY TOURS

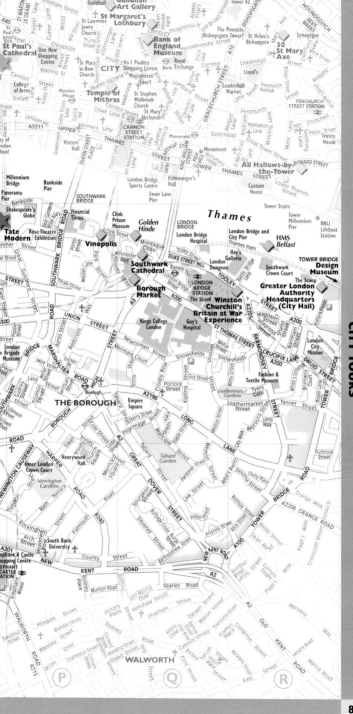

South Bank Quick Reference Guide

 SIGHTS AND EXPERIENCES

London Eye (▷ 28)

On a clear day you can see some 40km (25 miles) from the top of the giant wheel, right across London and as far as Windsor Castle (▷ 79). The Eye can carry 800 passengers per revolution and, with some three and a half million people stepping on board every year to enjoy the bird's-eye views, it is the most popular paid tourist attraction in Britain.

Tate Modern (▷ 54)

At the foot of the Millennium Bridge and presenting a distinctive face to the Thames, Tate Modern welcomes nearly five million visitors each year. The building itself, a converted power station, is almost as fascinating as the art within. The five-storey high Turbine Hall originally housed the electricity generators and the big spaces suit the art installations well.

MORE TO SEE	64

Borough Market
City Hall
Design Museum
Golden Hinde
Hayward Gallery
HMS *Belfast*
Imperial War Museum
SEA LIFE London Aquarium
Southwark Cathedral
Vinopolis
Winston Churchill's Britain at War Experience

Waterloo Bridge and Thames River Walkway

CITY TOURS

Fleet Street to the Tower

On this tour, see where the Romans founded Londinium in the first century AD and discover the city's long and fascinating history through its architecture, from Sir Christopher Wren's magnificent churches to the great Tower of London, with stories to capture everyone's imagination.

CITY TOURS

Morning
Arrive early at **St. Paul's Cathedral** (right, ▷ 44–45) before the crowds descend to appreciate fully its magnificence. The cathedral opens for sightseeing at 8.30am, but there are services, usually at 7.30am and 8am, which you could attend. The branch of the pâtisserie **Paul** in St. Paul's Churchyard is the perfect place for to stop for a snack.

Mid-morning
Walk up St. Martin's Aldersgate to the **Museum of London** (left, ▷ 30–31) and spend some time exploring its excellent collection. Retracing your steps, turn left into Gresham Street. Ahead is **St. Lawrence Jewry Church**, with dark wooden pews and a gold-encrusted ceiling lit by chandeliers. Cross the Guildhall Square to visit the **Guildhall Art Gallery** (▷ 70).

Lunch
Walk down King Street and turn right into Cheapside for an early lunch at **The Café Below** (▷ 145) in the crypt of **St. Mary-le-Bow**, a Wren church with striking modern stained-glass windows. A statue of Captain John Smith (1580–1631), leader of the Virginia Colony at Jamestown, presides over the square.

After lunch begin to make your way to the Tower of London, turning down Bow Churchyard passage, then turning right into Bow Lane, lined with smart shops and eateries, to cross Watling Street. On the left is the **Guild Church of St. Mary Aldermary**. Step inside to admire the magnificent ceiling.

The ruins of the **Temple of Mithras** (▷ 75) stand firm amid the soaring glass-and-steel modernity of the City's financial institutions. Looking ahead you'll see the distinctive **30 St. Mary Axe** (▷ 66), known as 'The Gherkin'. Passing the great pillars of the **Mansion House**, with the Bank of England in view, do some window-shopping in the **Royal Exchange** (right, ▷ 126) before exploring the food stands in **Leadenhall Market** (▷ 125).

Afternoon

Head down Philpot Lane to the Thames, pausing to admire Wren's towering **Monument** (to the Great Fire of London) on your right. The riverside Customs House Walkway will lead you to the **Tower of London** (below, ▷ 58–59). Aim to arrive by 2pm. Ideally you will have pre-booked your entrance ticket to avoid the queues (lines). First, take a tour with one of the Yeoman Warders, then spend the rest of the afternoon soaking up the history.

Evening

Sit by the Thames and enjoy the views of Tower Bridge and the south bank of the river. Walk through to **St. Katharine Docks** (▷ 73) and stroll among the smart yachts in the marina. The renovated ware-houses there house a host of bars and restaurants in which to relax. Alternatively, take the Circle Line from Tower Hill to Farringdon for a gastropub experience at **The Peasant** (▷ 150).

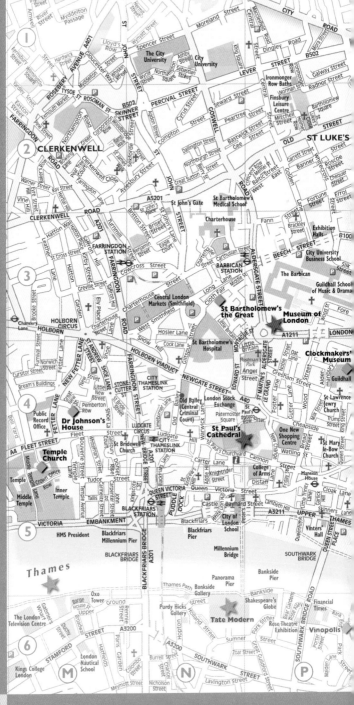

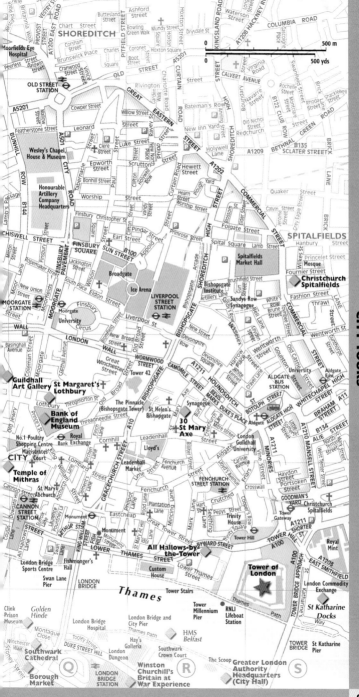

Fleet Street to the Tower
Quick Reference Guide

CITY TOURS

Museum of London (▷ 30)

There is no better place to get an overview of the city's history, from prehistoric times to the present day, than at this museum. Its fascinating exhibits are so well displayed, it would be hard not to be engrossed. The museum even stands where the city first began, on the site of the Roman fort.

St. Paul's Cathedral (▷ 44)

Five monarchs oversaw the building of Sir Christopher Wren's masterpiece, completed in 1710, and ever since it has been the place where events of national importance are celebrated, mourned and commemorated. Come in the early evening, to listen to the choir sing evensong.

Tower of London (▷ 58)

As it is one of London's most popular sights, it's definitely worth pre-booking your entry tickets for the Tower, especially during the high-season summer months. A tour with a Yeoman Warder (known as a Beefeater) as your guide is an experience that you'll always remember.

MORE TO SEE   **64**

30 St. Mary Axe
All-Hallows-by-the-Tower
Bank of England Museum
Christchurch Spitalfields
Clockmakers' Museum
Dr. Johnson's House

Guildhall Art Gallery
St. Bartholomew-the-Great
St. Margaret, Lothbury
St. Katharine Docks
Temple Church
Temple of Mithras

A new Routemaster bus outside St. Paul's

CITY TOURS

Covent Garden to Regent's Park

Literary associations, museums great and quirky, fine art and fun shopping all combine on this walk, which takes in busy streets and quiet corners. Here you'll find Theatreland, the heart of London's entertainment industry, and lively Chinatown.

Morning

From Holborn Underground station, turn off Kingsway to enter Lincoln's Inn Fields. On its northern side, **Sir John Soane's Museum** (left, ▷ 48–49) is wonderfully atmospheric. As you cross the leafy square, look to the left to see the impressive brick buildings of Lincoln's Inn, one of the Inns of Court, and ahead to the Royal College of Surgeons, where the **Hunterian Museum** (▷ 71) is located. **The Terrace in the Fields**, in Lincoln's Inn Fields, may tempt you to a coffee before continuing on to **The Old Curiosity Shop**, built in 1567, immortalized by Charles Dickens and now displaying handmade shoes. Following St. Clement's Lane will take you through the London School of Economics' campus and out alongside the Royal Courts of Justice to the Strand, where Wren's **St. Clement Danes Church** sits on an island amid busy traffic.

Mid-morning

Continue west along the Strand to **Somerset House** (▷ 50–51) to admire the great courtyard and immerse yourself in French Impressionist art at the **Courtauld Gallery** (below, ▷ 51).

Lunch

Eat lunch in grand surroundings in Somerset House or walk up Wellington Street into lively **Covent Garden**, which is packed with cafés, restaurants and bars. **Joe Allen** (▷ 148) is a favourite. Turn left for the **Piazza** (▷ 69). Here you can shop and enjoy the buzz in the former market (right). Cross Long Acre for the trendy shops on Neal Street.

Afternoon

Passing the brightly coloured high-rise blocks on St. Giles High Street, visit **St. Giles-in-the-Fields**, a handsome church with a Palladian interior, founded by Queen Matilda in 1101 as a leper hospital. Continue down Denmark Street, famed for its music connections, and cross Charing Cross Road with Foyles, London's most famous bookshop, on the left, to reach leafy **Soho Square**. In the 17th century, this was one of the most fashionable places to live. Today the area is home to the film and recording industries and numerous pubs and restaurants.

Mid-afternoon

Leave at Frith Street, go right at the Dog and Duck pub and stop for refreshment as you zigzag your way through cobbled Meard Street and across Wardour Street to the lively fruit and textiles **market** on Berwick Street. A left turn on Broadwick Street and another left down Lexington Street will take you among the specialist shops of Brewer Street and back onto Wardour Street. Cross Shaftesbury Avenue and turn left into Gerrard Street, the start of **Chinatown**.

Evening

Stroll through **Chinatown** (right) and pick a restaurant that takes your fancy. Shaftesbury Avenue is the heart of **Theatreland**, **Piccadilly Circus** is a short walk away and **Soho** buzzes with restaurants and nightlife.

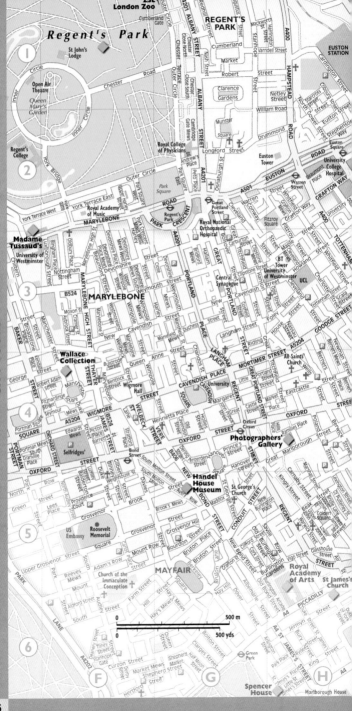

ZSL London Zoo

REGENT'S PARK

Regent's Park

St John's Lodge

EUSTON STATION

Open Air Theatre

Queen Mary's Garden

Regent's College

Chester Road

Clarence Gardens

Euston Tower

University College Hospital

Royal College of Physicians

Park Square

Royal Academy of Music

Royal National Orthopaedic Hospital

MARYLEBONE

Madame Tussaud's

University of Westminster

Central Synagogue

BT Tower University of Westminster

UCL

MARYLEBONE

Wallace Collection

All Saints' Church

Wigmore Hall

Cavendish Square

University

Photographers' Gallery

Selfridges'

Handel House Museum

St George's Church

US Embassy

Roosevelt Memorial

MAYFAIR

Church of the Immaculate Conception

Royal Academy of Arts

St James's Church

PICCADILLY

Green Park

Spencer House

Marlborough House

0 — 500 m

0 — 500 yds

96

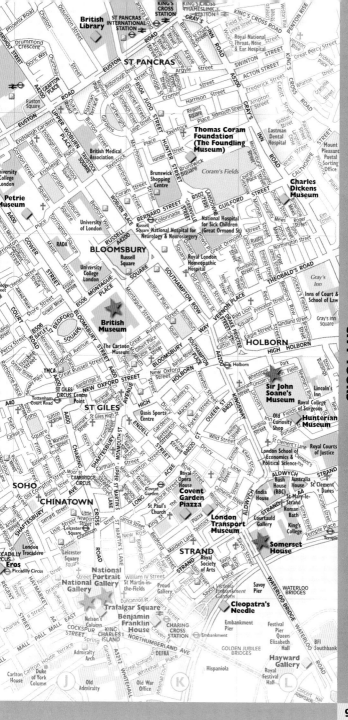

Covent Garden to Regent's Park
Quick Reference Guide

CITY TOURS

British Museum (▷ 16)
This is one of the world's greatest museums, where you can travel the globe through exhibits from every civilization. With eight million artefacts in the collection, you may find you visit more than once.

Sir John Soane's Museum (▷ 48)
Of all London's quirky small museums this one tops the bill, with architect Sir John Soane's eclectic collection packing every surface of his former home.

Somerset House (▷ 50)
In summer, fountains play in the courtyard; in winter it becomes an outdoor ice rink. Whenever you visit, there's likely to be something happening, and the art collection at the Courtauld Gallery is superb.

MORE TO SEE	64

British Library
Charles Dickens Museum
Cleopatra's Needle
Covent Garden Piazza
Eros
Foundling Museum
Handel House Museum

Hunterian Museum
London Transport Museum
Madame Tussaud's
Petrie Museum
Photographers' Gallery
Regent's Park and ZSL London Zoo
Wallace Collection

SHOP 118

Art and Antiques
Contemporary Applied Arts
Grays Antique Market
Books
Forbidden Planet
Stanfords
Department Stores
Liberty
Selfridges
Fashion
Brown's

Food and Drink
Villandry
Health and Beauty
Neal's Yard Remedies
Homeware
Aram Designs Ltd
Benjamin Pollock's Toyshop
Heal's
Thomas Goode Ltd

ENTERTAINMENT 128

Clubs
The Borderline
Guanabara
Salsa!
Jazz
Jazz After Dark
Pizza Express Jazz Room
Smollensky's on the Strand

Opera, Ballet and Concerts
London Coliseum
Royal Opera House
Wigmore Hall
Theatres
Donmar Warehouse
Theatre Royal, Drury Lane

EAT 140

Asian
Benares
Chaopraya Eat-Thai
Imli
Masala Zone
Rasa Samudra
Brasseries/Brunch
Christopher's
Joe Allen
British and Modern
Rules
European
Gaby's Deli
Hibiscus
Villandry
Wild Honey

Famous Chefs
The Square
Fish and Vegetarian
World Food Café
Gastropubs/Bars
Detroit
Lowlander
Lighter Bites
Paul

Westminster and St. James's

Westminster Abbey, the Houses of Parliament, Buckingham Palace, Trafalgar Square—some of London's most famous landmarks are located in Westminster. Follow in the footsteps of royalty as you take in famous art galleries, London's prettiest royal park and some upscale shopping.

Morning
Begin your day at **Trafalgar Square** (▷ 75), where Sir Edwin Landseer's lions proudly protect Nelson's Column. Presiding over its northern side, the **National Gallery** (▷ 32–33) shows Western European art in a stately setting. Next door, the **National Portrait Gallery** (above, ▷ 34–35) puts faces to famous names down the centuries. Both galleries have good cafés, but you may also like the nearby **Café in the Crypt** at **St. Martin-in-the-Fields** (▷ 138). Perhaps book for a candlelit concert while you are there.

Mid-morning
Walk down Whitehall to visit the **Banqueting House** (right, ▷ 14–15), noted for its Rubens ceiling, and to see the colourful **Horse Guards** and **Cenotaph** war memorial. You soon arrive at **Big Ben** and the **Houses of Parliament** (▷ 22–23). There are splendid views of the River Thames from Westminster Bridge, immortalized by poet William Wordsworth and Impressionist Claude Monet. **Westminster Abbey** (▷ 62–63) lies across the square.

Lunch
Turn up Storey's Gate to **St. James's Park** (▷ 42–43), perhaps picking up a sandwich en route to eat in this pretty royal park. Alternatively, try **Inn the Park** (▷ 148). You will pass the **Churchill War Rooms** (▷ 68) beneath a sweeping flight of steps, watched over by the statue of an imperious Clive of India, and may wish to return there after lunch. Stroll among the park's trees and flowerbeds and watch the ducks, geese, pelicans and interesting waterfowl on the lake.

Afternoon

Crossing the Mall, a wide ceremonial route packed with crowds on great occasions, you will see **Buckingham Palace** (above, ▷ 18–19) on your left, fronted by the Queen Victoria Memorial. Walk up the Mall to get a closer look at the palace, or cross to Marlborough Road alongside the red-brick **St. James's Palace.** A working royal palace, setting for official receptions, it houses the Household Office of Prince William and Prince Harry. **Clarence House** (▷ 68), home of Prince Charles and the Duchess of Cornwall, is on the far side of the palace.

Mid-afternoon

St. James's Street is lined with old-established businesses like wine-merchants **Berry Bros & Rudd** (▷ 123). Turn right into Jermyn Street for more quintessentially British shops, many carrying the Royal Warrant. Walking through the elegant Piccadilly Arcade brings you into Piccadilly, where **Fortnum & Mason** (▷ 124) is perfect for afternoon tea. **Hatchards** (▷ 125), booksellers since 1797, is next door. Visit **St. James's, Piccadilly** (▷ 73), Wren's church for the local aristocracy. There may be a concert on there in the evening.

Evening

If you like the Grand Café tradition, **The Wolseley** (▷ 151) is for you. Or dress up for a meal at **Greenhouse** (▷ 147) in Mayfair. Alternatively, reserve an evening Thames River **dinner cruise** (left, ▷ 56–57).

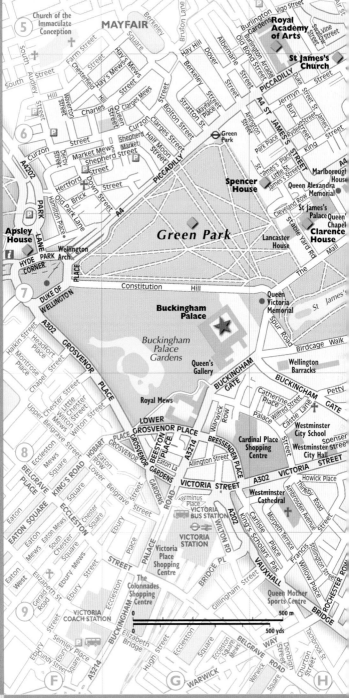

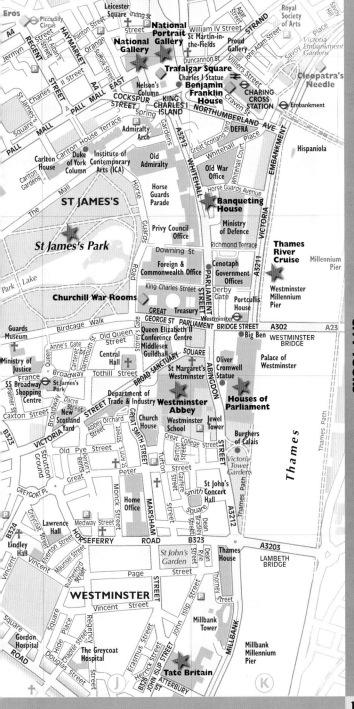

Westminster and St. James's
Quick Reference Guide

Banqueting House (▷ 14)
Inigo Jones's 17th-century architectural masterpiece has a magnificent Rubens ceiling.

Buckingham Palace (▷ 18)
The summer opening of this royal residence and office of the Royal Household is not to be missed.

Houses of Parliament (▷ 22)
Britain is governed from this landmark Victorian Gothic building on the banks of the Thames.

National Gallery (▷ 32)
The superb collection gives a over-view of European painting from Giotto to Cézanne.

National Portrait Gallery (▷ 34)
The famous and the infamous, past and present, are portrayed in paintings and photographs.

St. James's Park (▷ 42)
Tree-filled, surrounded by palaces and with a lake at its heart, this is the prettiest of the royal parks.

Tate Britain (▷ 52)
Tate Britain exhibits British art from 1500 to the 21st century, with a whole gallery devoted to Turner.

Thames River Cruise (▷ 56)
Sit down, relax and enjoy views of some of the most beautiful and interesting buildings in London.

Westminster Abbey (▷ 62)
The vast abbey is full of exquisite
detail and monuments. Herein lies
a pageant of British history.

Around Hyde Park

A feast of world-class museums and music put South Kensington firmly on every visitor's must-see list. Adjoining Hyde Park, Kensington Gardens come complete with a romantic royal palace and memories of Diana, Princess of Wales, who lived there.

Morning

At **South Kensington Underground** station there's a passage marked 'To the Museums'. Follow it, or come up to street level for a fortifying breakfast at one of the many cafés and pâtisseries that crowd this popular area. You are heading for the Cromwell Road and three world-class museums: the **Victoria and Albert Museum** (left, ▷ 60–61), the **Natural History Museum** (▷ 36–37) and the **Science Museum** (▷ 46–47). They are free, so you could pop into each one to get an idea of their riches, or spend the morning engrossed in the subjects that interest you most.

Mid-morning

All three museums have **cafés** to retreat to for sustenance. The café at the V&A is located in what was the world's first museum restaurant, in rooms intended as a showpiece of modern design and craftsmanship. During summer you can eat outdoors. The cafés at the Science and Natural History Museums are particularly child-friendly.

Lunch

Walk up Exhibition Road towards **Hyde Park** (▷ 71), turning left at Prince Consort Road to view the stately red-brick **Royal College of Music** and to approach the elliptical **Royal Albert Hall** (▷ 137). The **Café Consort** upstairs is a good lunch spot and you could perhaps make reservations for a concert or tour. Look at the detail on the frieze that rings this distinctive domed building and, going west, don't miss the reliefs and *sgraffito* that decorate the facade of the building opposite, previously occupied by the Royal College of Organists.

Afternoon

Cross Kensington Gore to the **Albert Memorial** (right, ▷ 66), an ornate fantasy by George Gilbert Scott, its glittering gold freshly restored. Stroll through **Kensington Gardens** to the Diana, Princess of Wales Memorial Fountain in adjacent Hyde Park. Then take the path back through Kensington Gardens via the Round Pond to **Kensington Palace** (▷ 24–25).

Mid-afternoon

Tour Kensington Palace and take afternoon tea in **The Orangery** (▷ 149). Leaving by the Kensington Palace Gardens exit and 'billionaires' row' of embassies, cross Kensington Church Street to the specialist shops and galleries along **Holland Street**. Turn left down **Kensington Church Walk** for exquisite little shops, courtyard houses and gardens. This is secret, village-like London yet only seconds away from busy Kensington High Street.

Dinner

Babylon (▷ 144), with its rooftop gardens and fabulous views across London, is nearby, as is Kensington favourite **Maggie Jones's** (▷ 148). Or you could take the bus to Knightsbridge, go shopping and relax in the **Champagne Bar** at **Harrods** (below, ▷ 124).

5

QUEENSWAY
Moscow Road
Bayswater
Queensborough Terrace
Craven Hill
Craven Hill
Mews
CRAVEN HILL
Craven
Lancaster
Mews
LANCASTER
TERRACE
WESTBOURNE
STREET
Porchester Terrace
Poplar Place
INVERNESS
PLACE
INVERNESS TERRACE
Leinster Mews
LEINSTER TERRACE
Lancaster
Gate
Elms
Mews
Lancaster
Gate
Westbourne
Gate
Caroline
Place
Queens
Ice Rink &
Bowl
B411
B411
Leinster
Gardens
Marlborough
Gate
Orme
Court
Queensway
ROAD
Black Lion
Gate
Portchester
Gate
Lancaster
Gate
BAYSWATER
A402
Inverness
Terrace Gate

6

Jubilee
Walk
The Broad Walk
Kensington
Speke's
Monument
Peter Pan
Statue
*Kensington
Gardens*
Physical
Energy
Statue
Round
Pond
Serpentine
Gallery
West Carriage Drive

7

KENSINGTON
CHURCH
STREET
Palace Gardens
Palace Avenue
The Broad Walk
**Kensington
Palace**
Palace
Gate
**Albert
Memorial**
Alexandra
Gate

KENSINGTON ROAD
HYDE PARK GATE
Kensington
Market
Young
Street
Kensington
Square
Thackeray St
St Alban's Grove
Cambridge
Place
Albert
Place
Douro Place
Canning Pl
Kensington
Court
Kensington
De Vere Gardens
Victoria Grove
PALACE GATE
Resto
Hyde Park Gate
Kensington
Gate
Queen's Gate
Queen's Gate
Jay Mews
Prince Consort Road
KENSINGTON GORE
Royal College
of Art
Royal
Albert
Hall
Royal
Geographical
Society
Albert Court
Exhibition
Imperial College
of Science
Royal College
of Music
Ayrton Road
Unwin Road
Queen's Gate

KENSINGTON

8

Stanford Rd
Cottesmore
Gardens
Eldon Road
Victoria Rd
Launceston
Place
Queen's Gate Terrace
Petersham
Place
Elvaston
Place
Petersham
Mews
Elvaston
Mews
Queen's Gate Mews
Gloucester Rd
Imperial College
Imperial College Road
Imperial College
Frankland
Road
Hyde Park
Chapel
**Science
Museum**
Earth
Galleries

Cornwall
Gardens
Cornwall
Gardens
Kynance
Mews
Petersham
Mews
GLOUCESTER ROAD
Queen's Gate
Queen's Gate
Place
Queen's Gate Place Mews
Queen's Gate
Gardens
**Natural History
Museum**
ROAD
A4

Lexham
Gardens
Emperor's Gate
Grenville
Place
Southwell
Gardens
B325
Southwell
Gardens
CROMWELL
Queensberry
Place
THURLOE

Cromwell
Hospital
Superstore
A4
CROMWELL
ROAD
Gloucester
Road
Ashburn
Gardens
Atwood Road
West Gloucester
Road
Stanhope
Gardens
Stanhope
Gardens
Harrington Road
Bute St
A3218
ROAD
South
Kensington

9

Courtfield
Gardens
Collingham
Courtfield
Gardens
Ashburn
Courtfield
Road
Gardens
Harrington
Gardens
Stanhope Gardens
Reece Mews
Harrington Road
B304

Hesper Mews
Colbeck
Mews
**SOUTH
KENSINGTON**
Wetherby Gardens
Bina
Gardens
Rosary
Gardens
Clareville
Grove
BROMPTON
Cranley
Place
Onslow
Square
Onslow

0 _____ 500 m
0 _____ 500 yds

(A)   (B)   OLD

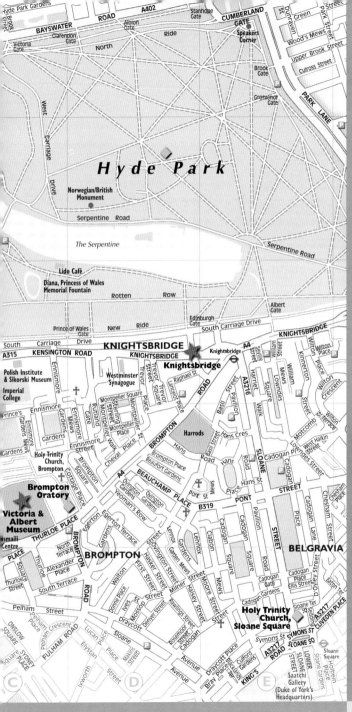

Around Hyde Park Quick Reference Guide

Kensington Palace and Gardens (▷ 24)

This historic royal palace, set in the 110ha (275-acre) Kensington Gardens, was home to Queen Victoria and more recently Diana, Princess of Wales.

Knightsbridge Shopping Spree (▷ 26)

Knightsbridge's shops enthral the most dedicated fashionista, with window displays to delight the eye. Don't miss London landmarks Harvey Nichols and Harrods.

Natural History Museum (▷ 36)

With everything that you have ever wanted to know about the natural world and a whole lot more under one roof, the museum is a truly fascinating place.

Science Museum (▷ 46)

With exhibits ranging from Stephenson's steam locomotive *Rocket* to a space capsule, and with an IMAX cinema and plenty of hand's-on fun, the museum makes science entertaining.

Victoria and Albert Museum (▷ 60)

This wonderful treasure house of decorative arts, one of the largest collections of its kind in the world, delights, inspires and often surprises.

CITY TOURS

111

Further Afield

Birthplace of Henry VIII and Elizabeth I, home to the National Maritime Museum and famed for the Royal Observatory, Greenwich (▷ 20–21) makes a great escape from central London, with open parkland, river views and a lively market selling food and crafts.

Morning
The perfect way to travel to Greenwich is by boat, as the royals did in centuries past, for the **Old Royal Naval College** (above, ▷ 20) presents a splendid baroque facade to the river. Alternatively, the Docklands Light Railway (DLR) gets you there quickly. Make your first stop the **Discover Greenwich** tourist information centre, which has an excellent exhibition on the **Maritime Greenwich World Heritage Site** and the very good **Old Brewery** café/bar (tel 0203 327 1280). Located in the Pepys Building, it is close to the magnificent *Cutty Sark*, the world's last tea clipper, restored after serious fire damage.

Mid-morning
Cross Romney Road to visit the **National Maritime Museum** (right, ▷ 21) and delve into all matters nautical, with plenty of hands-on exhibits. A colonnade links the museum with the elegant Palladian-style **Queen's House**, designed by Inigo Jones in the 17th-century. Today it houses a fine art collection that works by Gainsborough, Reynolds and Turner. Back across Romney Road, visit the neo-classical **Chapel of St. Peter and St. Paul** and the magnificent **Painted Hall** of the Old Royal Naval College. The ceiling here took 19 years to complete and the artist, James Thornhill, was eventually knighted for his labours. It was here that the body of Admiral Lord Nelson lay in state after the Battle of Trafalgar.

Lunch
There's a good **restaurant** downstairs in the Old Royal Naval College, or for something less formal, return to the **Old Brewery** in the Pepys Building.

Afternoon
Now head up the hill in Greenwich Park to the **Royal Observatory** (above, ▷ 96), commissioned by Charles II and designed by Wren in 1675 with the purpose of finding longitude at sea. The Time Galleries' exhibits, interactive **Astronomy Centre** and the **Peter Harrison Planetarium** are fascinating. Here you can stand astride the **Greenwich Meridian** line.

Mid-afternoon
Covering 74ha (183 acres) **Greenwich Park** is the oldest enclosed royal park, with rose gardens, a flower garden, lake, wilderness deer park and fine views across the Thames to Docklands and the City of London (left). Follow a path leading to Regency houses on Crooms Hill and continue downhill to the lively weekend **market**, packed with food stalls, crafts and small design shops.

Dinner
Take the DLR to **Canary Wharf** (▷ 76), in the heart of Docklands, to eat at the 18th-century waterside pub **The Gun** (▷ 147), once the haunt of smugglers and Lord Nelson's favourite trysting place.

Stanmore

Edgeware

A410

A409

A5

A4140

A404

A4005

A406

A40

Fryent
Country
Park

Wembley

Willesden

A404

Kilburn

Paddington

Wormwood
Scrubs

M1

A1

Finchley

Alexandra
Park

A406

A1000

Hendon

A1

A5

**Kenwood
House**

Golders
Hill Park

**Hampstead
Heath**

A41

Primrose
Hill

**Jewish
Museum**

EALING

A4020

A40

**Portobello
Road Market**

CITY

Kensington
Gardens

Hyde Park

Green
Park

A4020

M4

Holland
Park

HAMMERSMITH

WESTMINSTER

←Windsor

2

1

**Chiswick
House**

A4

**Chelsea
Physic
Garden**

Battersea
Park

Syon
Park

Kew
Gardens

**Royal
Botanic
Gardens, Kew**

**London
Wetland
Centre**

Thames

A316

RICHMOND

Richmond
Park

Putney

WANDSWORTH

Clapham

A3

Clapham
Common

Wandsworth
Common

Tooting
Bec
Common

**Ham
House**

Ham
Common

A307

A308

Wimbledon
Common

A3

A24

A214

Streatham

A216

Bushy
Park

KINGSTON
UPON THAMES

Wimbledon

A238

MERTON

**Hampton
Court Palace**

Hampton
Court Park

A309

Morden

Morden
Park

Morden
Hall
Park

Mitcham

Mitcham
Common

Poulter
Park

A24

A217

A3

A240

A243

A232

A231

SUTTON

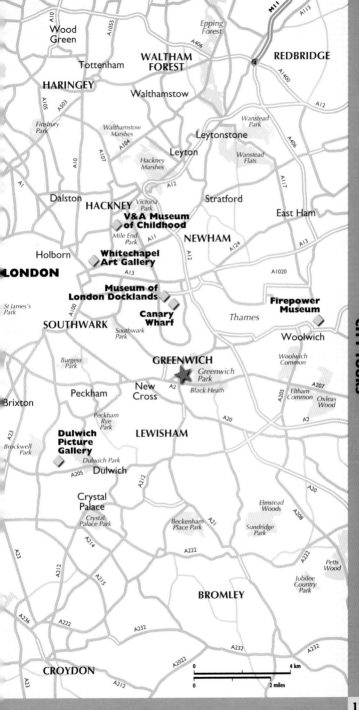

Wood Green

Tottenham

WALTHAM FOREST

Epping Forest

REDBRIDGE

HARINGEY

Walthamstow

Finsbury Park

Walthamstow Marshes

Wanstead Park

Leytonstone

Leyton

Wanstead Flats

Dalston

Hackney Marshes

HACKNEY

Victoria Park

Stratford

East Ham

NEWHAM

V&A Museum of Childhood

Mile End Park

Holborn

LONDON

Whitechapel Art Gallery

St James's Park

Museum of London Docklands

SOUTHWARK

Canary Wharf

Southwark Park

Firepower Museum

Thames

Woolwich

Burgess Park

GREENWICH

Greenwich Park

Woolwich Common

Brixton

Peckham

New Cross

Black Heath

Eltham Common

Oxleas Wood

Peckham Rye Park

LEWISHAM

Dulwich Picture Gallery

Dulwich Park

Dulwich

Brockwell Park

Crystal Palace

Crystal Palace Park

Beckenham Place Park

Elmstead Woods

Sundridge Park

Petts Wood

Jubilee Country Park

BROMLEY

CROYDON

0   4 km

0   2 miles

Further Afield Quick Reference Guide

TOP 25 SIGHTS AND EXPERIENCES

Greenwich (▷ 20)

The ideal way to spend a Sunday is to take a cruise on the Thames to Greenwich, a UNESCO World Heritage Site. Visit the great maritime sights and the Royal Observatory, take a leisurely stroll in historic Greenwich Park and shop in the lively crafts market.

Portobello Road Market (▷ 38)

Dedicate a Saturday to exploring the shops and stalls of an antiques market like no other. Whatever you're looking for, be it glass, china, curios or jewellery, it's likely you'll find it here and searching for treasure and bargaining with the dealers is all part of the fun.

Royal Botanic Gardens, Kew (▷ 40)

Flowers, trees, plants and shrubs from around the globe grow in swathes across landscapes and fill giant glasshouses in the world's most famous botanical garden. Take the treetop walkway for a bird's eye view.

MORE TO SEE   64

Canary Wharf
Chelsea Physic Garden
Chiswick House
Dulwich Picture Gallery
Firepower Museum
Ham House
Hampstead Heath
Jewish Museum

Kenwood House
London Wetland Centre
Museum of London Docklands
V&A Musuem of Childhood
Whitechapel Art Gallery

CITY TOURS

Shop

Whether you're looking for the best local products, a department store or a quirky boutique, you'll find them all in London. In this section shops are listed alphabetically.

SHOP

Introduction

If England really is a nation of shop-keepers, then London is the head office. You can find almost anything if you are determined enough. London has long been the world's marketplace and you'll find saris and spices as easily as rare reggae records, depending on the district—it really pays to explore beyond the West End. For shoppers, the choice ranges from vibrant street markets to legendary department stores and from offbeat boutiques to smart galleries of paintings and antiques.

Contemporary and Traditional

It is the range that excites visitors, whether in antiques, classics or cutting-edge contemporary. London has outrageous fashion, bolstered by the annual crop of imaginative art-, fashion- and design-school graduates. By contrast, long-established shopping streets, such as Oxford Street and Kensington High Street, offer mass-market goods, while markets such as Camden Lock and Portobello Road are eclectic, ethnic and inexpensive.

Buying a London Memory

London's souvenirs range from tatty to tasteful. Ever since the Swinging Sixties, anything with a

---

BEST OF BRITISH

Take home some British souvenirs with a difference. You can buy beautifully crafted umbrellas and walking sticks from James Smith & Sons (✉ 53 New Oxford Street, WC1). For a good British cheese buy a Stilton, all ready and packed, from Paxton & Whitfield (✉ 93 Jermyn Street, SW1). If you want to try some British recipes go to Books for Cooks (✉ 4 Blenheim Crescent, W11) for a large selection of cookbooks. Tea addicts should head to the Tea House (✉ 15A Neal Street, WC2) for a choice of blends and some stylish teapots. English herbs, oils and toiletries from Culpeper Herbalists (✉ 8 The Market, Covent Garden, WC2) make great presents.

Clockwise from top: The elegant arcades of Leadenhall Market; handmade shoes for sale in St. James's; one of the antiques shops in Camden Passage; the central well

Union Jack flag on it has sold well. For high quality, go to the museum shops. Gifts at the shop in Buckingham Palace Mews include the Queen Victoria range of china, a mini-throne for a charm bracelet or a guardsman puppet. The Victoria and Albert Museum, British Museum and National Gallery also stock quality items inspired by their diverse collections— budget permitting, you can do a full-scale family gift shop at any of these. The Design Museum offers chic designer goods, while the Museum of London is particularly good for souvenirs and books about London. At the National Portrait Gallery, you will find books on historical figures and British history, as well as a good supply of postcards and posters.

The Ultimate British Buy

Go to St. James's or Knightsbridge to purchase traditional British-made goods such as tweed jackets, handmade shoes or delicate fragrances, elegant china, floral printed fabrics and cashmere sweaters. Visit Burlington Arcade (▷ panel below) for its specialist upscale shops in a historic setting. Burberry and Aquascutum are synonymous with raincoats. Harrods has been trading for some 150 years; Selfridges was the country's first department store; and Liberty fabrics are still exotic and luxurious. Their January and July sales are major events on any serious shopper's calendar.

SHOP THE SHOP

Charles Dickens would recognize many London shops. Burlington Arcade, off Piccadilly, is an 18th-century covered shopping mall, with a liveried beadle to maintain decorum. Many shops display the royal insignia, showing that they supply members of the Royal Household with everything from brushes to jewels (www.royalwarrant. org). For instance, John Lobb (✉ 88 Jermyn Street, SW1) custom-makes shoes and boots for the royal family—and for you, at a price.

in Liberty; Lobb on St. James's Street, selling exclusive made-to-measure shoes; Fortnum & Mason in Piccadilly, renowned for its luxury foods and top-notch wines

SHOP

Directory

Fleet Street to the Tower

Street Markets
Leadenhall Market
Petticoat Lane
Spitalfields Market

Covent Garden to Regent's Park

Art and Antiques
Contemporary Applied Arts
Grays Antique Market
Books
Forbidden Planet
Stanfords
Department Stores
Liberty
Selfridges
Fashion
Brown's
Food and Drink
Villandry
Health and Beauty
Neal's Yard Remedies
Homeware
Aram Designs Ltd
Benjamin Pollock's Toyshop
Heal's
Thomas Goode Ltd

Westminster and St. James's

Art and Antiques
Agnews
Books
Hatchards
Department Stores
Fortnum & Mason
Fashion
Turnbull & Asser
Food and Drink
Berry Bros & Rudd

Around Hyde Park

Department Stores
Harrods
Harvey Nichols
Peter Jones
Fashion
Jimmy Choo
Lulu Guinness
Urban Outfitters
Homeware
Jeanette Hayhurst

Further Afield

Books
Books for Cooks
Fashion
Brora
Food and Drink
Rococo
Homeware
Ceramica Blue
Designers Guild
Shopping Centres
Westfield London
Street Markets
Bermondsey Market
Camden Markets

Shopping A–Z

AGNEWS

www.agnewsgallery.com

This internationally renowned art gallery, in business since 1817, specializes in European Old Masters and British art from the 17th to the 20th centuries.

🚇 G6 ✉ 35 Albermarle Street, W1 ☎ 020 7290 9250 🕓 Mon–Fri 10–5.30, Sat by appointment 🚇 Green Park

ARAM DESIGNS LTD

www.aram.co.uk

Aram's international modern designs are displayed on five floors. Stock includes furniture, lighting and glass.

🚇 K4 ✉ 110 Drury Lane, WC2 ☎ 020 7557 7557 🕓 Mon–Sat 🚇 Covent Garden

BENJAMIN POLLOCK'S TOYSHOP

www.pollocks-coventgarden.co.uk

Selling traditional toy theatres and collectable toys for adults and children, this toy shop is delightfully different.

🚇 K5 ✉ 44 The Market, WC2 ☎ 020 7379 7866 🕓 Daily 🚇 Covent Garden

BERMONDSEY MARKET

www.bermondseysquare.co.uk

Rise before dawn on a Friday and join the antiques-hunters at Bermondsey Market. The market is best for small items.

PRIVATE GALLERIES

An indispensable tool for visitors getting to grips with commercial art galleries in London is the monthly *Galleries* magazine (www.galleries.co.uk), which is available free from most galleries. With its maps and specialist subject index, information can be called up by area as well as subject.

🚇 R8 ✉ Bermondsey Square, SE1 🕓 Fri 4am–1pm ☎ 020 7525 6000 🚇 London Bridge

BERRY BROS & RUDD

www.bbr.com

Wine merchant Berry Bros & Rudd has traded in the same shop since 1698. Prices range from around £5 to £5,000. The own-label bottles are good value.

🚇 H6 ✉ 3 St. James's Street, SW1 ☎ 0800 280 2440 🕓 Mon–Sat. Closed bank holidays 🚇 Green Park

BOOKS FOR COOKS

www.booksforcooks.com

Browse the amazing selection of books about cooking and cuisine, then head to the café, where recipes are tested. Cookery classes are held in the demonstration kitchen.

🚇 Off map ✉ 4 Blenheim Crescent, W11 ☎ 020 7221 1992 🕓 Tue–Sat. Closed Good Fri, bank holidays, last 3 weeks in Aug, Christmas and New Year 🚇 Ladbroke Grove

BRORA

www.brora.co.uk

Choose from cashmere in an array of shades for men, women and children. It is pricey, but the quality is superb.

🚇 Off map ✉ 344 King's Road, SW3 ☎ 020 7352 3697 🕓 Daily 🚇 Sloane Square

BROWNS

www.brownsfashion.com

This boutique has long led the fashion pack, offering chic designs at grown-up prices.

🚇 F4 ✉ 23–27 South Molton Street, W1 ☎ 020 7514 0000 🕓 Mon–Sat 🚇 Bond Street

BOOKSHOP CAFÉS

Bookshop cafés to seek out include the cake shop connected by a passage in the History section of London Review Bookshop (✉ 14 Bury Place, WC1 ☎ 020 7269 9030) and the café next to the Jazz department of Foyles (✉ 113–19 Charing Cross Road, WC2 ☎ 020 7437 5660). Waterstone's superstore on Piccadilly has a café, a juice bar and a restaurant with great views.

CAMDEN MARKETS
www.camdenlock.net
The small, vibrant market at Camden Lock has expanded and spawned other markets, from the Underground station up to Hawley Road. The market is famous for alternative and vintage fashion.
➕ Off map ✉ Camden High Street to Chalk Farm Road, NW1 ⏰ Daily 9.30–6 with more stalls at weekends ⓜ Camden Town

CERAMICA BLUE
www.ceramicablue.co.uk
With imaginative design and a feast of colour for the table and kitchen, hand-picked from designers worldwide, Ceramica Blue is good for unusual gifts.
➕ Off map ✉ 10 Blenheim Crescent, W11 ☎ 020 7727 0288 ⏰ Daily ⓜ Ladbroke Grove, Notting Hill Gate

CONTEMPORARY APPLIED ARTS
www.caa.org.uk
For quality contemporary crafts in central London, head to CAA, which is dedicated to promoting British artists.
➕ J3 ✉ 2 Percy Street, W1 ☎ 020 7436 2344 ⏰ Mon–Sat ⓜ Tottenham Court Road

DESIGNERS GUILD
www.designersguild.com
Tricia Guild's store is a wonderland of exquisite design, with a range of modern china, glass and fabrics.
➕ Off map ✉ 277 King's Road, SW3 ☎ 020 7351 5775 ⏰ Mon–Sat ⓜ Sloane Square, then a 15 min walk or bus 19 or 22

FORBIDDEN PLANET
www.forbiddenplanet.com
This megastore sells a wide range of fantasy, horror and science fiction, as well as comic books.
➕ J4 ✉ 179 Shaftesbury Avenue, WC2 ☎ 020 7420 3666 ⏰ Daily ⓜ Tottenham Court Road

FORTNUM & MASON
www.fortnumandmason.com
Before going in London's premier grocer's shop, do not miss the clock, which has Messrs. Fortnum and Mason mincing forward each hour. The shop-brand Fortnum's goods make perfect presents.
➕ H6 ✉ 181 Piccadilly, W1 ☎ 020 7734 8040 ⏰ Daily ⓜ Piccadilly Circus, Green Park

GRAYS ANTIQUE MARKET
www.graysantiques.com
High-quality goods ranging from silver to vintage fashion are sold by over 200 dealers.
➕ F5 ✉ 1–7 Davies Mews and 58 Davies Street, W1 ☎ 020 7629 7034 ⏰ Mon–Sat ⓜ Bond Street

HARRODS
www.harrods.com
This vast emporium contains just about everything anyone could want. Don't miss the food halls.
➕ D8 ✉ 87–135 Brompton Road, SW1 ☎ 020 7730 1234 ⏰ Daily ⓜ Knightsbridge

HARVEY NICHOLS

www.harveynichols.com

Harvey Nichols bags the title of London's classiest clothes shop. It has a chic, popular restaurant.

➕ E7 ✉ 109–125 Knightsbridge, SW1 ☎ 020 7235 5000 🕐 Daily 🚇 Knightsbridge

HATCHARDS

www.hatchards.co.uk

Hatchards well-informed staff still know how to make book-buying a rewarding experience.

➕ H6 ✉ 187 Piccadilly, W1 ☎ 020 7439 9921 🕐 Daily 🚇 Piccadilly Circus, Green Park

HEAL'S

www.heals.co.uk

A front-runner of the 1920s Arts and Crafts movement, Heal's specializes in timeless contemporary furniture and homewares.

➕ J3 ✉ 196 Tottenham Court Road, W1 ☎ 020 7636 1666 🕐 Daily 🚇 Goodge Street

JEANETTE HAYHURST

www.antiqueglass-london.com

One of the few places to find old glass, especially British pieces, this shop also stocks studio glass.

➕ Off map ✉ 32a Kensington Church Street, W8 ☎ 020 7938 1539 🕐 Mon–Fri 🚇 High Street Kensington

AUCTION HOUSES

A visit to one of London's auction houses, even just to view, is an experience: try Bonham's (✉ 101 New Bond Street, W1 ☎ 020 7447 7447; www.bonhams.com), Christie's (✉ 8 King Street, SW1 ☎ 020 7839 9060; www.christies.com) or Sotheby's (✉ 34 New Bond Street, W1 ☎ 020 7293 5000; www.sothebys.com).

JIMMY CHOO

www.jimmychoo.com

A fashionista heaven, Jimmy Choo in Knightsbridge is the place to buy the highest-heeled designer shoes in town.

➕ E7 ✉ 32 Sloane Street, SW3 ☎ 020 7823 1051 🕐 Daily 🚇 Knightsbridge

LEADENHALL MARKET

www.leadenhallmarket.co.uk

This surprising City treat is housed under architect Horace Jones's 19th-century arcades, with quality food shops and pubs.

➕ R4 ✉ Leadenhall, EC3 🕐 Mon–Fri 7–4 🚇 Bank, Monument

Vibrant Camden Lock Market

LIBERTY

www.liberty.co.uk

Offering everything from sumptuous fabrics to china and glass, this shop's quality is characterized by exoticism and cutting-edge fashion mixed with an Arts and Crafts heritage all brought together in a beautiful mock-Tudor building.

➕ G4 ✉ Regent Street, W1 ☎ 020 7734 1234 ⏰ Daily 🚇 Oxford Circus

LULU GUINNESS

www.luluguinness.com

Selling 1950s-style handbags, hats and shoes, this sleek, modern shop is popular with celebrities. There is a second branch in the City's Royal Exchange.

➕ E9 ✉ 3 Ellis Street, SW1 ☎ 020 7823 4828 ⏰ Mon–Sat 🚇 Sloane Square

NEAL'S YARD REMEDIES

www.nealsyardremedies.com

Committed to using natural ingredients in its products for over 30 years, Neal's Yard health and beauty shop is a Covent Garden institution.

➕ K4 ✉ 15 Neal's Yard, WC2 ☎ 020 7379 7222 ⏰ Daily 🚇 Covent Garden

PETER JONES

www.johnlewis.com

Shopping in this high-quality Sloane Square department store is a pleasure. There are great views from the café and cocktail bar.

➕ E9 ✉ Sloane Square, SW1 ☎ 020 7730 3434 ⏰ Daily 🚇 Sloane Square

PETTICOAT LANE

Petticoat Lane is the place to go if you're looking for clothing at bargain prices. It is best on Sunday.

➕ S4 ✉ Middlesex and Wentworth streets, E1 ⏰ Mon–Fri 10–4.30, Sun 9–2 🚇 Liverpool Street, Aldgate

ROCOCO

www.rococochocolates.com

The chocolates at this upscale chocolatier offer a taste sensation. Try the bars flavoured with Earl Grey tea, chilli pepper or nutmeg.

➕ Off map ✉ 321 King's Road, SW3 ☎ 020 7352 5857 ⏰ Daily 🚇 Sloane Square

ROYAL EXCHANGE

www.theroyalexchange.com

William Tite's City landmark is now a beautiful upscale shopping mall.

➕ Q4 ✉ Cornhill ⏰ Mon–Fri, times vary from shop to shop 🚇 Bank

SELFRIDGES

www.selfridges.com

Selfridges department store rivals Harvey Nichols (▷ 125) for day-long retail therapy. Don't miss the superb food hall.

➕ F4 ✉ 400 Oxford Street, W1 ☎ 0800 123 400 ⏰ Daily 🚇 Marble Arch, Bond Street

SPITALFIELDS MARKET

www.visitspitalfields.com

Wander among the craft stalls and array of food outlets. There is an organic section Friday and Sunday.

S3 ✉ Commercial Street, E1 ⏰ Mon–Fri 10–4, Sun 9.30–5 🚇 Liverpool Street

STANFORDS
www.stanfords.co.uk
With London's largest selection of maps, plus travel books and a good little café, Stanfords is a must for all travel enthusiasts.
K5 ✉ 12–14 Long Acre, WC2 ☎ 020 7836 1321 ⏰ Daily 🚇 Covent Garden

THOMAS GOODE LTD
www.thomasgoode.com
Collectors of bone china need look no further than this splendid showroom. Famous English names include Wedgwood, Minton, Spode & Royal Worcester.
F5 ✉ 19 South Audley Street, W1 ☎ 020 7499 2823 ⏰ Mon–Sat 🚇 Green Park, Bond Street

TURNBULL & ASSER
www.turnbullandasser.com
If you want classic British design, then the made-to-measure or off-the-peg shirts here are for you. Quality and service are superb.
H6 ✉ 71–72 Jermyn Street, SW1 ☎ 020 7808 3000 ⏰ Mon–Sat 🚇 Green Park, Piccadilly Circus

URBAN OUTFITTERS
www.urbanoutfitters.co.uk
Check out the latest trends in streetwear and accessories at this branch of Urban Outfitters.
Off map ✉ 36–38 Kensington High Street, W8 ☎ 020 7761 1001 ⏰ Daily 🚇 High Street Kensington

VILLANDRY
www.villandry.com
This quality 'foodstore' sells French and English cheeses, great breads, olive oil, charcuterie and more.

G3 ✉ 170 Great Portland Street, W1N ☎ 020 7631 3131 ⏰ Daily 🚇 Great Portland Street

WESTFIELD LONDON
http://uk.westfield.com/london
With over 300 shops, spanning designer and high-street labels, department stores and specialist boutiques, Westfield provides an all-day shopping experience. In 2011, the larger Westfield Stratford City, by the Olympic site, opened.
Off map ✉ Ariel Way, W12 ☎ 020 3371 2300 🚇 Shepherd's Bush, Wood Lane

Liberty's mock-Tudor main entrance

Entertainment

Once you've done with sightseeing for the day, you'll find lots of other great things to do with your time in this chapter, even if all you want to do is relax with a drink. In this section establishments are listed alphabetically.

Introduction

When darkness falls, London's pace doesn't let up, as eager visitors join Londoners in the capital's lively nightclubs, bars and pubs. Licensing laws were revised in 2006, permitting many venues, from pubs to clubs, to stay open longer. The smoking ban of 2007, however, saw smokers relegated to the pavement.

Entertainment

London's Theatreland, with its lavish West End musicals and plays starring A-list actors, is famed worldwide, but there's a great deal happening in smaller venues all over town, including alternative theatre, comedy and cabaret. Hundreds of concerts take place every week in a variety of buildings, but especially churches, where the quality of lunchtime and evening recitals is very high and admission either nominal or free. There are opera, ballet and modern dance seasons in memorable locations, too, plus an array of fun festivals, especially during the school holidays and long public holiday weekends.

Film

As well as the big-screen cinemas in the West End showing the latest blockbuster movies, London has some very good venues screening art-house and indie films. The BFI Southbank

WALK THE WALK

The 2km-long (1 mile) stretch of riverside on the South Bank between Westminster Bridge and London Bridge bustles by night, as well as by day. The London Eye is magical after dusk. On the opposite bank, illuminated landmarks include the Houses of Parliament and Somerset House. At Oxo Tower Wharf, go to the top floor for a drink or a meal—there are few better views of London. Admire Tate Modern (open until 10pm Friday and Saturday) and the Globe. Rest your feet at a riverside pub and enjoy spectacular views.

Clockwise from top: The Garrick Theatre in the West End; the Theatre Royal on Haymarket; the BFI IMAX on the South Bank; Shakespeare's Globe, a re-creation of

(▷ 133), which hosts the annual London Film Festival in October, Ciné Lumière (▷ 134), the Electric Cinema in Notting Hill (www.electriccinema.co.uk), the Curzon Mayfair and Renoir in the Brunswick Centre (both www.curzoncinemas.com) are all well worth visiting.

Summer Living

In the summer, London's outdoors comes into its own. Londoners enjoy concerts in beautiful settings such as Hampton Court Palace, Kenwood House, Hyde Park and Kew Gardens, often bringing picnics with them. The music ranges from classical and opera to jazz and rock. In summertime, bars, pubs and cafés spill onto the city's streets, and many serve good food.

Clubs, Pubs and Bars

Year-round, the diversity of the club scene is legendary, and with many changing themes, check before you go. There are tried-and-tested venues and a host of pulsing new wave options. London's extensive bar scene ranges from cocktails at the elegant Savoy or the see-and-be-seen Blue Bar at The Berkeley (▷ 156) to Irish bars, sports bars and traditional street-corner pubs. Some are in warrens of Tudor rooms; others take pride in their grand Victorian and Edwardian decorations.

SUPERSIZE CLUBBING

Find Friday and Saturday night Las Vegas-style, gaudy glam parties for 2,600 at Proud2 (✉ The O2, Peninsula Square, SE10 ☎ 020 8463 3070; www.proud2.com), where you can expect live music, DJ sets, burlesque and circus performers through to 7am. Under Blackfriars Bridge on the Southbank, Ibiza-sized Pulse (✉ Southwark Street, SE1 ☎ 020 7403 9643; www.pulseclub.co.uk) is London's largest state-of-the-art club space, complete with signature hi-tech sound and video mapping.

---

an Elizabethan playhouse; Young Dancer, a bronze by Enzo Plazzotta outside the Royal Opera House in Covent Garden; jazz musicians play in the popular Dover Street

Directory

South Bank

Clubs
Ministry of Sound
Film
BFI IMAX
BFI Southbank
Opera, Ballet and Concerts
Purcell Room
Queen Elizabeth Hall
Royal Festival Hall
Theatres
National Theatre
Old Vic
Shakespeare's Globe
Young Vic

Fleet Street to the Tower

Clubs
Fabric
Events
Broadgate Centre
Opera, Ballet and Concerts
Barbican Concert Hall
Theatres
Barbican Centre Theatre

Covent Garden to Regent's Park

Clubs
The Borderline
Guanabara
Salsa!
Jazz
Jazz After Dark
Pizza Express Jazz Room
Smollensky's on the Strand
Opera, Ballet and Concerts
London Coliseum
Royal Opera House
Wigmore Hall
Theatres
Donmar Warehouse
Theatre Royal, Drury Lane

Westminster to St. James's

Bars
Trader Vic's
Clubs
Dover Street
Comedy
The Comedy Store
Dancing
The Ritz
Film
Institute of Contemporary Arts (ICA)
Opera, Ballet and Concerts
St. James's, Piccadilly
St. Martin-in-the-Fields

Around Hyde Park

Film
Ciné Lumière
Opera, Ballet and Concerts
Cadogan Hall
Holland Park Theatre
Royal Albert Hall
Theatres
Royal Court/Jerwood Theatre Upstairs

Further Afield

Clubs
606 Club
Barfly
Bush Hall
Koko

Notting Hill Arts Club
O2 Academy Brixton
Scala
Events
O2 Arena
Wembley
Jazz
Bull's Head, Barnes
Jazz Café
Opera, Ballet and Concerts
Sadler's Wells Theatre
Sport
All England Lawn Tennis Club, Wimbledon
Kia Oval
Lord's Cricket Ground
Wembley

Entertainment A–Z

606 CLUB

www.606club.co.uk

West London's best small jazz club books musicians with impeccable credentials. Alcohol is served only with food and the music cover charge is added to the cost of the meal.

Off map ✉ Lots Road, SW10 ☎ 020 7352 5953 🕐 Sun–Thu 7pm–1am, Fri–Sat 8pm–2am Ⓔ Earl's Court, Fulham Broadway

ALL ENGLAND LAWN TENNIS CLUB, WIMBLEDON

www.wimbledon.com

In late June, line up for tickets to tennis's top tournament (advance tickets only for the last four days). Tours and museum entrance are available all year.

Off map ✉ Church Road, SW19 ☎ Tours: 020 8946 6131 Ⓔ Southfields

BARBICAN CENTRE THEATRE

www.barbican.org.uk

Currently an exciting mix of domestic and international companies play seasons here.

P3 ✉ Barbican Centre, Silk Street, EC2 ☎ 020 7638 8891 Ⓔ Barbican

BARBICAN CONCERT HALL

www.barbican.org.uk.

Home to the London Symphony Orchestra and the BBC Symphony Orchestra, the Barbican also welcomes visiting orchestras, singers and soloists.

R3 ✉ Barbican Centre, Silk Street, EC2 ☎ 020 7638 8891; range of good ticket deals Ⓔ Barbican

BARFLY

www.barflyclub.com

A Camden club that hosts more than 20 indie groups a week—some bad, some OK and some destined for stardom.

Off map ✉ 49 Chalk Farm Road, NW1 ☎ 020 7688 8994 🕐 Mon–Thu 3pm–midnight, Fri–Sat 3pm–3am, Sun 7pm–midnight Ⓔ Chalk Farm

BFI IMAX

www.bfi.org.uk/imax

Watch exhilarating 2-D and 3-D movies in this 500-seat cinema in a space-age setting.

L6 ✉ 1 Charlie Chaplin Walk, South Bank, SE1 ☎ 020 7199 6000 Ⓔ Embankment, Waterloo

BFI SOUTHBANK

www.bfi.org.uk

BFI Southbank screens a diverse range of films and is the focus of the annual London Film Festival.

L6 ✉ South Bank, SE1 ☎ 020 7928 3232 Ⓔ Embankment, Waterloo

THE BORDERLINE

www.meanfiddler.com

The hottest indie and rock bands strut their stuff at the venerable Borderline club in the West End.

J4 ✉ Orange Yard, off Manette Street, W1 ☎ 020 7734 5547 🕐 Club: Mon–Fri 11pm–3am, Sat–Sun 11pm–4am. Shows: 7pm–10.30pm Ⓔ Tottenham Court Road

---

THEATRE TIPS

If you care about where you sit, go in person and peruse the plan. For an evening 'sold out' performance, it is worth waiting in line for returns; otherwise, try for a matinée. The most inexpensive seats may be far from the stage or uncomfortable, so take binoculars and a cushion. Londoners rarely dress up for the theatre any more but they do order their intermission drinks before the play starts, and remain seated while they applaud.

London is full of music. At lunchtime, the best places are churches, where concerts are usually free. Try St. Anne and St. Agnes, and St. Olave's in the City; St. James's, Piccadilly; and St. Martin-in-the-Fields in Trafalgar Square. St. Paul's Cathedral has choral evensong at 5pm Monday to Saturday, 3.15 on Sunday. Look for concerts in historic houses, museums and galleries, especially during the City of London Festival (July). On summer evenings music is played outside in the Embankment Gardens or at Kenwood House (▷ 77).

The famed Comedy Store

BROADGATE CENTRE

www.broadgateinfo.net

This amphitheatre surrounded by bars, restaurants and shops provides a schedule of summer entertainment and a winter ice rink.
➕ R3 ✉ Broadgate Circus, Eldon Street, EC2 ☎ 020 7505 4010 Ⓣ Liverpool Street

BULL'S HEAD, BARNES

www.thebullshead.com

Enjoy good jazz in the friendly atmosphere of a riverside pub.
➕ Off map ✉ 373 Lonsdale Road, SW13 ☎ 020 8876 5241 Ⓞ Mon–Sat 8.30pm–11pm, Sun 1–3.30, 8.30–11 Ⓡ Barnes Bridge

BUSH HALL

www.bushhallmusic.co.uk

Listen to jazz, rock, folk or classics performed by famous names and upcoming artists at this ornate Edwardian dance hall.
➕ Off map ✉ 310 Uxbridge Road, Shepherd's Bush, W12 ☎ 020 8222 6955 Ⓞ Shows: 7.30pm, see website for listings Ⓡ Shepherd's Bush Market

CADOGAN HALL

www.cadoganhall.com

This concert hall off Sloane Square is home to the Royal Philharmonic Orchestra. It also welcomes visiting musicians and vocalists.
➕ E9 ✉ 5 Sloane Terrace, SW1 ☎ 020 7730 4500 Ⓣ Sloane Square

CINÉ LUMIÈRE

www.institut-francais.org.uk

Part of the French government's hub of language and culture, Ciné Lumière shows French films and other European and world cinema.
➕ B9 ✉ Institut Français, 17 Queensberry Place, SW7 ☎ 020 7073 1350 Ⓣ South Kensington

THE COMEDY STORE

www.thecomedystore.co.uk

The best in stand-up comedy features improvised sketches from the Comedy Store Players. Many big names in British TV and radio have cut their teeth here.
➕ J5 ✉ 1a Oxendon Street, SW1 ☎ 0844 871 7699 Ⓞ Doors open Sun–Thu at 6.30pm, Fri–Sat 6pm. Show times vary, check website for details Ⓣ Piccadilly Circus, Leicester Square

DONMAR WAREHOUSE
www.donmarwarehouse.com
The Donmar Warehouse attracts adventurous theatregoers to its avant-garde productions.
➕ J4 ✉ 41 Earlham Street, WC2 ☎ 0844 871 7624 Ⓜ Covent Garden

DOVER STREET
www.doverstreet.co.uk
Music at this large, popular basement, bedecked with candles, can be jump jive, jazz, rhythm and blues or Big Band. The food is good. Dress code is smart casual.
➕ G6 ✉ 8–10 Dover Street, W1 ☎ 020 7629 9813 Ⓒ Restaurant: Mon–Thu 6pm–2am, Fri–Sat 7pm–2am. Club: Mon–Sat 10pm–3am Ⓜ Piccadilly Circus, Green Park

FABRIC
www.fabriclondon.com
This fabulously cool superclub is known for its music blasted out in three rooms and is hugely popular.
➕ N3 ✉ 77a Charterhouse Street, EC1 ☎ 020 7336 8898 Ⓒ Sat–Sun 11pm–8am, Fri 10pm–6am Ⓜ Farringdon

GUANABARA
www.guanabara.co.uk
Grab a *caipirinha* and salsa onto the dance floor at this Brazilian-themed venue. Tables must be booked in advance.
➕ K4 ✉ Parker Street, WC2 ☎ 020 7242 8600 Ⓒ Mon–Sat 5pm–2.30am, Sun 5pm–midnight Ⓜ Covent Garden, Holborn

HOLLAND PARK THEATRE
www.operahollandpark.com
Confusingly, this is highly acclaimed opera, not theatre, which is staged in summer (June to August) beneath a canopy in one of London's most lush and romantic parks.

➕ Off map ✉ Holland Park, W8 ☎ 0845 230 9769 Ⓜ Holland Park, High Street Kensington

INSTITUTE OF CONTEMPORARY ARTS (ICA)
www.ica.org.uk
Founded by a collective of artists, poets and writers, the Institute of Contemporary Arts hosts cutting-edge art, screens seriously arty films and plays host to performance artists charting new territory in all media.
➕ J6 ✉ The Mall, SW1 ☎ 020 7930 3647 Ⓜ Piccadilly Circus, Charing Cross

JAZZ AFTER DARK
www.jazzafterdark.co.uk
Jazz and blues attract a keen young crowd. The cocktails are good and the food simple.
➕ J4 ✉ 9 Greek Street, W1 ☎ 020 7734 0545 Ⓒ Tue–Thu 5pm–1.30am, Fri–Sat 5pm–2.30am Ⓜ Tottenham Court Road

JAZZ CAFÉ
www.jazzcafelive.com
Buzzing nightly with the widest range of jazz, from soul to rap, this is a popular spot for the young.
➕ Off map ✉ 5 Parkway, NW1 ☎ 020 7688 8899 (restaurant); 0870 060 3777 (tickets) Ⓒ Mon–Sun 7pm–2am Ⓜ Camden Town

KIA OVAL

www.kiaoval.com

The Oval is where Surrey County Cricket Club play home games. It is also a venue for test cricket and Sunday league games.

➕ Off map ✉ Surrey County Cricket Club, Kennington, SE11 ☎ 08712 461100 🚇 Oval

KOKO

www.koko.uk.com

Since 1890, this Camden Town venue has been through many incarnations. Today, go for hip-hop, trance, pop, rock and partying under the gigantic mirror ball.

➕ Off map ✉ 1a Camden High Street, NW1 ☎ 0870 432 5527 🕐 Sun–Thu 7pm–11.30pm, Fri 7pm–10pm. Club NME: Fri 10pm–4am, Sat 9pm–4am 🚇 Mornington Crescent, Camden Town

LONDON COLISEUM

www.eno.org

The London Coliseum is home to the English National Opera (ENO), which is known for exciting and innovative productions.

➕ J5 ✉ St. Martin's Lane, WC2 ☎ 0871 911 0200 🚇 Leicester Square, Charing Cross

TICKET TIPS

Use the 'tkts' half-price ticket booth (in Leicester Square). Preview tickets and matinée tickets have reduced prices. Get up early and line up for one-day bargain tickets at the RNT and RSC. Go with friends and make a party booking at a reduced rate. Ask the National Theatre, Royal Court and other theatres about special discounts on particular performances; and keep student and senior citizen cards ready. Remember, the show is the same wherever you sit!

LORD'S CRICKET GROUND

www.lords.org

Lords is the home of the MCC (Marylebone Cricket Club) and is where Middlesex play home games. The ground hosts test cricket, major finals and Sunday league games.

➕ Off map ✉ St. John's Wood Road, NW8 ☎ 020 7616 8500 🚇 St. John's Wood

MINISTRY OF SOUND

www.ministryofsound.com

This legendary club is housed in a prison-like building.

➕ N8 ✉ 103 Gaunt Street, SE1 ☎ 020 7378 6528 🕐 Fri 10.30pm–6.30am, Sat 11pm–7am (last entry 4.30am) 🚇 Elephant and Castle

NATIONAL THEATRE

www.nationaltheatre.org.uk

Home of the National Theatre company, the National Theatre has three performance spaces; the Olivier, Lyttelton and Cottesloe. All stage several productions in repertory.

➕ L6 ✉ South Bank, SE1 ☎ 020 7452 3000 Information, tickets and tours 🚇 Embankment, Waterloo 🚆 Waterloo

NOTTING HILL ARTS CLUB

www.nottinghillartsclub.com

Diversity and originality results from artists and DJs meeting here and swapping ideas.

➕ Off map ✉ 21 Notting Hill Gate, W11 ☎ 020 7460 4459 🕐 Times vary, check website for details 🚇 Notting Hill Gate

O2 ACADEMY BRIXTON

www.o2academybrixton.co.uk

South London's favourite live music venue attracts big-name bands. It has an art deco interior and room for nearly 5,000 on the

The Royal Opera House, Covent Garden (☎ 020 7304 4000; www.roh.org.uk) has 90-minute backstage tours and a 45-minute Velvet, Gilt and Glamour tour. Front-of-house tours of the Royal Albert Hall (☎ 0845 401 5045; www.royalalberthall.com) last an hour and the guides have some great stories. The National Theatre tours are always highly praised (☎ 020 7452 3400; www.nationaltheatre.org.uk), and actors lead you through history at the Theatre Royal, Drury Lane (☎ 0844 412 2705; www.theatreroyal.co.uk).

huge sloping dance floor. All the big rock bands have played and recorded here.
➕ Off map ✉ 211 Stockwell Road, SW9 ☎ 020 7771 3000 🕙 Times vary, check website for details 🚇 Brixton, Stockwell

O2 ARENA
www.theo2.co.uk
A music and sports venue in former Millennium Dome, the O2 Arena has a capacity of 20,000.
➕ Off map ✉ Peninsula Square, SE10 ☎ 0871 984 0002 🚇 North Greenwich

OLD VIC
www.oldvictheatre.com
This sumptuous theatre stages critically acclaimed productions.
➕ M7 ✉ The Cut, Waterloo Road, SE1 ☎ 0844 871 7628 🚇 Waterloo, Southwark

PIZZA EXPRESS JAZZ ROOM
www.pizzaexpress.com
Savour quality pizzas and great jazz in this friendly Soho cellar (booking essential). Other branches have live jazz, too.
➕ J4 ✉ 10 Dean Street, W1 ☎ 020 7437 9595 🚇 Tottenham Court Road

PURCELL ROOM
www.southbankcentre.co.uk
Listen to chamber music, singers and musicians and more in this intimate space.
➕ L6 ✉ South Bank, SE1 ☎ 0844 875 0073 🚇 Embankment, Waterloo

QUEEN ELIZABETH HALL
www.southbankcentre.co.uk
Come here for small orchestras, choirs, small-scale opera, piano recitals and dance.
➕ L6 ✉ South Bank, SE1 ☎ 0844 875 0073 🚇 Embankment, Waterloo

THE RITZ
www.theritzlondon.com
To enter a bygone world, dress up for dinner and a dance on a Friday or Saturday at London's most opulent dining room (booking essential). For a more modest experience, go for afternoon tea or to the Rivoli Bar.
➕ G6 ✉ 150 Piccadilly, W1 ☎ 020 7493 8181 🚇 Green Park

ROYAL ALBERT HALL
www.royalalberthall.com
Sporting events fill the 6,000-seat hall as successfully as the annual 'Prom' season (the Henry Wood Promenade Concerts), which runs from mid-July to mid-September, offering nightly concerts and cheap 'prom' tickets to stand or sit on the floor of the pit.
➕ B7 ✉ Kensington Gore, SW7 ☎ 0845 401 5045 🚇 South Kensington

ROYAL COURT/JERWOOD THEATRE UPSTAIRS
www.royalcourttheatre.com
The Royal Court has a lofty artistic reputation and presents only new

ENTERTAINMENT

work by leading or emerging playwrights. In the 1950s, John Osbourne's *Look Back In Anger* shook up London theatre forever, and today's productions follow in its wake. The main theatre seats 400, the studio 60.

E9 ⊠ Sloane Square, SW1 ☎ 020 7565 5000 Sloane Square

ROYAL FESTIVAL HALL
www.southbankcentre.co.uk
The Royal Festival Hall, at the heart of the South Bank Centre arts complex, stages world-class performances, with large-scale orchestral concerts, plus jazz and ballet.

L6 ⊠ South Bank, SE1 ☎ 0844 875 0073 Embankment, Waterloo

ROYAL OPERA HOUSE
www.roh.org.uk
The opulent Royal Opera House in Covent Garden is home to the Royal Ballet and is an evocative setting for grand opera.

K5 ⊠ Bow Street, Covent Garden, WC2 ☎ 020 7304 4000 Covent Garden

SADLER'S WELLS THEATRE
www.sadlerswells.com
Sadler's Wells is one of the most electrifying dance theatres in Europe, with international and British companies presenting innovative dance of all genres.

M1 ⊠ Rosebery Avenue, EC1 ☎ 020 7863 8198 Angel

ST. JAMES'S, PICCADILLY
www.st-james-piccadilly.org
Sir Christopher Wren's mid-17th century church makes a sumptuous setting for lunchtime and evening choral and orchestral concerts, plus star lecturers.

H6 ⊠ 197 Piccadilly, W1 ☎ 020 7734 4511 Piccadilly Circus

ST. MARTIN-IN-THE-FIELDS
www.stmartin-in-the-fields.org
Baroque music is the focus of the free lunchtime concerts (Monday, Tuesday and Friday) and candlelit evening concerts (Thursday, Friday and Saturday). There are also jazz nights in the crypt, where there's a popular, good-value café/restaurant.

K5 ⊠ Trafalgar Square, WC2 ☎ 020 7839 8362 Leicester Square

SALSA!
www.barsalsa.info
Dance the night away after a salsa class held in the bar, and eat some delicious Latin American food as you practise.

J5 ⊠ 96 Charing Cross Road, WC2 ☎ 020 7379 3277 Mon–Sat 5.30pm–2am, Sun 5.30pm–1am Tottenham Court Road

SCALA
www.scala-london.co.uk
This King's Cross superclub is spread over four main floors, with a viewing gallery. Music is provided

---

PUB MUSIC

This can be one of the least expensive and most enjoyable evenings out in London, worth the trip to an offbeat location. For the price of a pint of beer (usually a huge choice) you can settle down to enjoy the ambience and listen to some of the best alternative music available in town—from folk, jazz and blues to rhythm and blues, soul and more. Audiences tend to be friendly, loyal to their venue and happy to talk music.

by DJs and live bands.
🚇 Off map ✉ Pentonville Road, N1
☎ 020 7833 2022 🕐 Live music nights:
7.30pm–11pm. Club nights: 9pm–3am
🚇 King's Cross

SHAKESPEARE'S GLOBE
www.shakespearesglobe.org
The performance season at this
reconstruction of an open-air
Elizabethan playhouse runs May to
September; take a coat and rainhat
to watch works by Shakespeare
and his contemporaries. Tours
operate year-round.
🚇 P6 ✉ 21 New Globe Walk, SE1 ☎ 020
7401 9919 🚇 London Bridge, Mansion
House

SMOLLENSKY'S ON THE STRAND
www.smollenskys.com
A pianist plays on week nights and
there is jazz on Sunday nights at
this American bar-restaurant.
🚇 K5 ✉ 105 The Strand, WC2 ☎ 020
7497 2101 🚇 Charing Cross

THEATRE ROYAL DRURY LANE
www.theatre-royal.com
The theatre, built in 1812, stages
mostly musicals. There are reput-
edly ghosts—the Man in Grey is
said to walk around the Upper
Circle.
🚇 K5 ✉ Catherine Street, WC2 ☎ 0870
890 1109 🚇 Covent Garden

TRADER VIC'S
www.tradervicslondon.com
The South Seas meet Park Lane in
this Tahitian-inspired bar in the
Hilton Hotel. It's pricey but fun, and
the tropical cocktails are a work of
art. The bar is open daily.
🚇 F6 ✉ 22 Park Lane, W1 ☎ 020 7208
4113 🚇 Hyde Park Corner

A production at Shakespeare's Globe

WEMBLEY
www.wembleystadium.com
www.livenation.co.uk/wembley
The state-of-the art football
stadium, where the English
national team plays home games,
also hosts big-name pop and rock
concerts.
🚇 Off map ✉ Stadium Way, Wembley,
Middlesex ☎ 0844 980 8001 🚇 Wembley
Park 🚇 Wembley Stadium

WIGMORE HALL
www.wigmore-hall.org.uk
The hall was built in 1901 as a
recital hall for Bechstein Pianos, so
it has perfect acoustics. It is one of
London's most beautiful settings
for recitals and chamber music,
especially for Sunday concerts.
🚇 F4 ✉ 36 Wigmore Street, W1 ☎ 020
7935 2141 🚇 Bond Street

YOUNG VIC
www.youngvic.org
Young directors stage innovative
productions of classic and new
plays and musicals here.
🚇 M7 ✉ The Cut, SE1 ☎ 020 7922 2922
🚇 Waterloo, Southwark

Eat

There are places to eat across the city to suit all tastes and budgets. In this section establishments are listed alphabetically.

EAT

Introduction

With more than 50 restaurants awarded one or more Michelin stars, the capital's reputation for fine dining continues to grow. Chefs have high profiles and London creates its own culinary trends. Using the finest-quality ingredients, modern British cuisine values simplicity and flavour, innovation and elegant presentation.

Cafés, Brasseries and Pubs

Multicultural London offers exciting restaurants serving a wide variety of different cuisines, ranging from European and cutting-edge contemporary to Indian, Asian and Middle Eastern. Tapas and sushi bars are popular and you don't have to look far to find a good spicy curry or fragrant Thai treat. No longer just an excuse to rest your feet, museum and art gallery cafés are as much of a destination as their exhibitions, and, with their all-day menus, convivial brasseries have a relaxed Continental air. Gastropubs combine a fine setting with quality drinks and food.

Fast Food and Restaurant Chains

Try the Gourmet Burger Kitchen, Yo!Sushi, Wagamama, All-Bar-One and Masala Zone. Zizzi and Pizza Express are good pizza chains.

Afternoon Tea

A great British institution, afternoon tea is still available in hotels and tearooms from about 2 or 3pm. It always includes a pot of tea and something to eat, which can vary from dainty sandwiches and cakes to scones with clotted cream and jam.

DRESS CODE

In the past the British loved to dress for dinner, but these days only the most formal restaurants demand a jacket and tie. Customers should dress appropriately, however, to eat in upscale restaurants.

Top to bottom: The Palm Court at the Ritz; summertime alfresco dining in the capital; focaccia for sale at Borough Market; artisan breads, Borough Market

Directory

South Bank

British and Modern
Oxo Tower Bar,
  Brasserie &
  Restaurant
European
Baltic
Blueprint Café
Cantina Vinopolis
Fish and Vegetarian
Livebait
Gastropubs/Bars
The Anchor
Anchor & Hope
Lighter Bites
Tate Modern Café

Fleet Street to the Tower

British and Modern
Cicada
Medcalf
St. John
European
Bevis Marks
  Restaurant
Club Gascon
Famous Chefs
Fifteen
Rhodes Twenty Four
Fish and Vegetarian
The Café Below
Gastropubs/Bars
The Peasant

Covent Garden to Regent's Park

Asian
Benares
Chaopraya Eat-Thai
Imli
Masala Zone
Rasa Samudra
Brasseries/Brunch
Christopher's
Joe Allen

British and Modern
Rules
European
Gaby's Deli
Hibiscus
Villandry
Wild Honey
Famous Chefs
The Square
Fish and Vegetarian
World Food Café
Gastropubs/Bars
Detroit
Lowlander
Lighter Bites
Paul

Westminster and St. James's

Asian
Tamarind
British and Modern
Portrait Restaurant
The Wolseley
Famous Chefs
Le Gavroche
Greenhouse
International
Gaucho
Lighter Bites
Inn the Park

Around Hyde Park

Asian
Amaya
Royal China
British and Modern
Babylon
Le Café Anglais
Maggie Jones's
Famous Chefs
Maze
Tom Aikens
Lighter Bites
The Orangery

Further Afield

British and Modern
The Glasshouse
Ottolenghi
European
Providores & Tapa
  Room
Gastropubs/Bars
The Gun

EAT

Eating A–Z

PRICES

Prices are approximate, based on a 3-course meal for one person.

£££	over £60
££	£30–£60
£	under £30

AMAYA ££

www.amaya.biz
Enjoy sophisticated Indian grills and curries in an upscale setting with a theatrical show kitchen.
➕ E8 ✉ Halkin Arcade, SW1 ☎ 020 7823 1166 🕐 Mon–Sat 12.30–2.15, 6.30–11.30, Sun 12.45–2.45, 6.30–10.30
🚇 Knightsbridge

THE ANCHOR £

This historic pub with black beams, a maze of tiny rooms and garden patio enjoys excellent river views. Food is traditional British, with fish and chips and Sunday roasts.
➕ P6 ✉ Bankside, 34 Park Street, SE1 ☎ 020 7407 1577 🕐 Restaurant: Mon–Sat 12–10, Sun 12–9.30 🚇 London Bridge

RIVERSIDE EATING

London is exploiting the potential of its riverside views. As well as traditional pubs like The Anchor (▷ above) many new restaurants are opening along the South Bank. The most spectacular views are from the Oxo Tower Restaurant (▷ 149) and Tate Modern's rooftop restaurant at Bankside (▷ 151). There are lower but impressive views from the Blueprint Café (▷ 145) beside the Design Museum, Butler's Wharf, overlooking Tower Bridge and the City. For a more modest river view, try the Barley Mow pub (✉ 44 Narrow Street, E14), which overlooks the wider, curving Thames of the East End.

ANCHOR & HOPE ££

A quality gastropub in a great building, the Anchor & Hope serves good British food. There are no reservations, so arrive early. Service can be slow.
➕ M7 ✉ 36 The Cut, SE1 ☎ 020 7928 9898 🕐 Tue–Sat 12–2.30, 6–10.30, Mon 6–10.30, Sun 12.30–5 🚇 Southwark, Waterloo

BABYLON ££

www.roofgardens.virgin.com
Take a seat in the amazing rooftop gardens, complete with oak trees, flamingos and expansive views over London, for elegant modern British cuisine. Being there is a great experience.
➕ Off map ✉ The Roof Garden, 99 Kensington High Street, W8 ☎ 020 7368 3993 🕐 Mon–Sat 12–2.30, 7–10.30, Sun 12–4 🚇 High Street Kensington

BALTIC £

www.balticrestaurant.co.uk
Head to the bar for some serious cocktails, then on to the dramatic contemporary restaurant for modern Polish and Eastern European food and jazz every Sunday 7pm.
➕ N6 ✉ 74 Blackfriars Road, SE1 ☎ 020 7928 1111 🕐 Restaurant: daily 12–3.30, 5.30–11.15. Bar: 12–12 🚇 Southwark

BENARES £££

www.benaresrestaurant.com
Atul Kochhar serves subtly spiced and stylishly presented Indian dishes in his Michelin-starred Mayfair restaurant. The menu is seasonally inspired, with innovative vegetarian options.
➕ G5 ✉ 12a Berkeley Square House, Berkeley Square, W1 ☎ 020 7629 8886 🕐 Daily 12–2.30, Mon–Sat 5.30–11, Sun 6–10.30 🚇 Green Park

BEVIS MARKS RESTAURANT ££

www.bevismarkstherestaurant.com
This kosher restaurant is next to the 18th-century synagogue. Israeli and other wines are on offer.
➕ R4 ✉ Bevis Marks, EC3 ☎ 020 7283 2220 🕐 Mon–Fri 12–3, Mon–Thu 5.30–10 🚇 Aldgate

BLUEPRINT CAFÉ ££

www.blueprintcafe.co.uk
Jeremy Lee's restaurant at the Design Museum serves up European dishes and stunning London views.
➕ S7 ✉ Design Museum, 28 Shad Thames, SE1 ☎ 020 7378 7031 🕐 Mon–Sat 12–3, 6–11, Sun 12–4 🚇 London Bridge

LE CAFÉ ANGLAIS £–££

www.lecafeanglais.co.uk
Rowley Leigh's vast but inviting art deco restaurant in the Whiteley's shopping centre attracts food-lovers with an unfussy menu, an open kitchen and oyster bar.
➕ A4 ✉ 8 Porchester Gardens, W2 ☎ 020 7221 1415 🕐 Restaurant: Mon–Thu 12–3.30, 6.30–10.30, Fri–Sat 12–3.30, 6.30–11, Sun 12–3.30, 6.30–10. Oyster Bar: Mon–Sat 12–10.30, Sun 12–10 🚇 Bayswater, Queensway

THE CAFÉ BELOW £

www.cafebelow.co.uk
Enjoy exceptional vegetarian food in an ancient Norman church crypt in the heart of the City.
➕ P4 ✉ St. Mary-le-Bow, Cheapside, EC2 ☎ 020 7329 0789 🕐 Mon–Fri 7.30am–9pm 🚇 Bank, St. Paul's, Mansion House

CANTINA VINOPOLIS ££

www.cantinavinopolis.com
At this vivacious, wine-themed restaurant and bar, Mediterranean-influenced dishes are prepared in an open kitchen.
➕ P6 ✉ 1 Bank End, SE1 ☎ 020 7940 8333 🕐 Mon–Wed 6pm–11pm, Thu–Fri 12–3, 6–11, Sat 12–11 🚇 London Bridge

CHAOPRAYA EAT-THAI ££

www.eatthai.net
Enjoy classic Thai dishes at this quiet, stylish restaurant just behind Oxford Street.
➕ F4 ✉ 22 St. Christopher's Place, W1 ☎ 020 7486 0777 🕐 Daily 12–3, 6–11 🚇 Bond Street

CHRISTOPHER'S ££

www.christophersgrill.com
One of the best places in London for a genuine American brunch, Christopher's is in a most beautiful Victorian town house dining room.
➕ K5 ✉ 18 Wellington Street, WC2 ☎ 020 7240 4222 🕐 Mon–Fri 7–10, 12–3, 5–11.30, Sat 11.30–3.30, 5–11.30, Sun 11.30–3.30, 5–10.30. Martini bar: Mon–Wed 11.30am–midnight, Thu–Sat 11.30am–1.30am 🚇 Covent Garden

EAT

CICADA £

www.rickerrestaurants.com

A popular minimalist bar/ restaurant serving Pan-Asian fusion food including dim sum, curries, sashimi and salads, Cicada attracts a stylish crowd who create a lively, fun atmosphere.

➕ N3 ✉ 132–136 St. John Street, EC1 ☎ 020 7608 1550 🕔 Mon–Fri 12–11, Sat 6–11 🚇 Farringdon

CLUB GASCON £££

www.clubgascon.com

Good for that special dinner, Club Gascon serves unusual, robust dishes from Gascony. Reserve well in advance.

➕ N3 ✉ 57 West Smithfield, EC1 ☎ 020 7796 0600 🕔 Mon–Fri 12–2, 7–10.30, Sat 7–10.30 🚇 Barbican, Farringdon

DETROIT £

www.detroit-bar.com

Retro decor, funky sounds and tempting cocktails feature at this established Covent Garden bar. The bar snacks menu includes burgers, vegetable tempura and a trio of houmous.

➕ K4 ✉ 35 Earlham Street, WC2 ☎ 020 7240 2662 🕔 Mon–Sat 5–midnight 🚇 Leicester Square

FIFTEEN ££

www.fifteen.net

At Fifteen, chef Jamie Oliver provides successful training for the unemployed. The mainly Italian cuisine is served in the Trattoria and in the open-kitchen restaurant downstairs. Booking is advised.

➕ Q1 ✉ 15 Westland Place, N1 ☎ 020 3375 1515 🕔 Mon–Sat 7.30–11, 12–3, 6.30–10, Sun 8–11, 12–3.30, 6.30–9.30 🚇 Old Street

GABY'S DELI £

Inspired by a New York Jewish diner, this is the place to head for no-nonsense food, either to eat in or to take out.

A classic double-decker club sandwich served with flair
Modern British cuisine uses the finest ingredients

J5 ✉ 30 Charing Cross Road, WC2
☎ 020 7836 4233 🕐 Mon–Sat 11am–
midnight, Sun 12–10pm 🚇 Leicester
Square

GAUCHO £££

www.gauchorestaurants.co.uk
Meat-eaters will relish the steaks
at this Argentinian restaurant and
wine bar. Or for a lighter meal, try
the tasty *ceviches* (marinated raw
fish. Excellent South American
wines complement the food. The
top floor has live music.
H5 ✉ 25 Swallow Street, W1 ☎ 020
7734 4040 🕐 Mon–Sat 12–12, Sun 12–11
🚇 Piccadilly Circus

LE GAVROCHE £££

www.le-gavroche.co.uk
Albert's Roux's son sticks to classic
French cuisine, but creates lighter
dishes. Enjoy amazing wines and a
grand setting.
E5 ✉ 43 Upper Brook Street, W1
☎ 020 7408 0881 🕐 Mon–Fri 12–2,
6.30–11, Sat 6.30–11 🚇 Marble Arch

THE GLASSHOUSE ££

www.glasshouserestaurant.co.uk
The perfect preamble to a walk in
Kew Gardens, the Glasshouse
serves notable modern dishes,
including ravioli of salmon, skate
with parsley, *beurre noisette*,
capers and raisins, and slow-
cooked pork cheeks with creamed
potatoes. Reserve in advance.
Off map ✉ 14 Station Parade, Kew
☎ 020 8940 6777 🕐 Mon–Thu 12–2.30,
7–10.30, Fri–Sat 12–2.30, 6.30–10.30, Sun
12.30–3, 7–10 🚇 Kew Gardens

GREENHOUSE £££

www.greenhouserestaurant.co.uk
Chef Antonin Bonnet serves
imaginative yet serious food,
complemented by superb wines.
Choose from the à la carte,
seasonal, vegetarian or tasting
menus and enjoy fine contemporary French cuisine that hasn't
forgotten its classic roots.
G6 ✉ 27a Hay's Mews, W1 ☎ 020
7499 3331 🕐 Mon–Fri 12–2.30, 6.30–11,
Sat 6.30–11 🚇 Green Park

THE GUN ££

www.thegundocklands.com
A popular, comfortable gastropub
on Canary Wharf, with stunning
views, Gun serves imaginative,
seasonal British food. Try the
Brixham plaice with aromatic
English samphire, Jersey Royal
potatoes and *buerre noisette*.
Off map ✉ 27 Coldharbour, Isle of
Dogs, E14 ☎ 020 7515 5222 🕐 Mon–Sat
11am–midnight, Sun 11–11 🚇 Canary
Wharf, Blackwall

HIBISCUS £££

www.hibiscusrestaurant.co.uk
Chef Claude Bosi's bold, inventive
modern French cooking gets rave
reviews.
G5 ✉ 29 Maddox Street, W1S ☎ 020
7629 2999 🕐 Tue–Thu 12–2.30, 6.30–10,
Fri–Sat 12–2.30, 6–10, Mon 6.30–10
🚇 Oxford Circus

EAT

THE BILL

When the bill (check) arrives, read it
carefully. A 12.5 per cent service charge,
or more, may have been added. If the
service you received has not been satisfac-
tory, or if you prefer to tip your waiter
personally in cash, ask them to remove it.
A hefty bill can quickly mount up, so, to
avoid any unpleasant surprises, check
whether VAT and coffee are included and
if there's a 'cover charge'. Order tap water
if you don't want to pay for bottled water.

The unmistakable OXO Tower

EAT

IMLI £–££
www.imli.co.uk
Contemporary Indian food, served tapas-style, is ideal for sharing.
➕ H4 ✉ 167–169 Wardour Street, W1F ☎ 020 7287 4243 🕐 Mon–Wed 12–11, Thu–Sat 12–11.30 🚇 Tottenham Court Road

INN THE PARK £
www.innthepark.com
Enjoy contemporary British food with lake and park views from the terrace. Tempting afternoon teas are served daily 3–4.30pm.
➕ J7 ✉ St. James's Park, SW1 ☎ 020 7451 9999 🕐 Mon–Fri 8am–11pm, Sat–Sun 9am–10pm 🚇 St. James's Park

JOE ALLEN ££
www.joeallen.co.uk
For healthy American Cal-Ital food head to this dependably convivial and clublike establishment. Reservations are essential.
➕ K5 ✉ 13 Exeter Street, WC2 ☎ 020 7836 0651 🕐 Mon–Fri 9am–12.45am, Sat 11.30am–12.45am, Sun 11.30am–11.45pm 🚇 Covent Garden

LIVEBAIT £
www.livebaitrestaurants.co.uk
The original Livebait restaurant near the Young and Old Vic theatres in The Cut serves simply presented fresh fish, shellfish and seafood. Try the queen scallop risotto, *moules marinières* or fresh tuna with sour cream and wasabi mash. The express menu is good value.
➕ M7 ✉ 43 The Cut, SE1 ☎ 020 7928 7211 🕐 Mon–Sat 12–11, Sun 12.30–9 🚇 Southwark

LOWLANDER £
www.lowlander.com
This Belgian bar and brasserie is well-located for a pre-theatre meal. Try the rib-eye *steak frites* or home-made fishcake salad.
➕ K4 ✉ 36 Drury Lane, WC2 ☎ 020 7379 7446 🕐 Mon–Wed 11.30–11, Thu–Sat 11.30–11.30, Sun 12–10.30 🚇 Covent Garden

MAGGIE JONES'S ££
This Kensington institution is much-loved for its informality, wine list and no-nonsense British food.
➕ Off map ✉ 6 Old Court Place, Kensington Church Street, W8 ☎ 020 7937 6462 🕐 Daily 12.30–2.30, 6.30–11 (Sun 10.30) 🚇 High Street Kensington

---

SET-PRICE MENUS

Many of London's pricier restaurants offer two set-price menus—lower in price at lunchtime. Try classic Anglo-French cuisine at the Connaught Grill (➕ E5 ✉ 16 Carlos Place, W1 ☎ 020 3147 7200) or lunch at Gordon Ramsey's Maze (▷ 149). Most of the star chefs offer these menus including Tom Aikins, Richard Corrigan and Philip Howard.

MASALA ZONE ££

www.masalazone.com

From the creators of Chutney Mary and Veeraswamy, both known for their authentic dishes, comes an informal setting for thalis and Indian street food. There are other branches in the capital.

🔲 H5 ✉ 9 Marshall Street, W1 ☎ 020 7287 9966 🕐 Mon–Sat 12–11.30, Sun 12.30–10.30 🚇 Oxford Circus

MAZE ££

www.gordonramsay.com/maze

Enjoy Gordon Ramsay's imaginative haute cuisine—French with Asian influences—in a wonderfully congenial atmosphere. The three- and four-course lunchtime set menus are competitively priced.

🔲 F5 ✉ 10–13 Grosvenor Square, W1 ☎ 020 7107 0000 🕐 Daily 12–2.30, 6–10.30 🚇 Bond Street

MEDCALF £–££

www.medcalfbar.co.uk

The carefully crafted British menu changes daily and respects top-quality ingredients.

🔲 M2 ✉ 40 Exmouth Market, EC1 ☎ 020 7833 3533 🕐 Mon–Thu 12–3, 6–9.45, Fri–Sat 12–3, 6–10.15, Sun 12–4. Bar: Mon–Sat 12–11, Sun 12–4 🚇 Farringdon

THE ORANGERY £

www.hrp.org.uk

An 18th-century building overlooking Kensington Palace's formal gardens creates the perfect setting for elegant light lunches or afternoon tea—cucumber sandwiches or scones with jam and cream.

🔲 A6 ✉ Kensington Palace, Kensington Gardens, W8 ☎ 0844 7777 🕐 Mar–Sep daily 10–6; Oct–Feb 10–5 🚇 High Street Kensington

---

INDIAN FOOD

London's 2,000 or so Indian restaurants cater to a well-informed local clientele. An Indian meal should have many dishes so, if you are a group, consider making a collective order and sharing. Tandoori dishes (cooked in a clay oven) make good starters. A North Indian meal's main course might include one or two meat offerings, two or three vegetable dishes, rice, a lentil or other pulse, and a variety of breads such as chapatti or naan—which are eaten hot, so order more as you go along. Remember the yogurt and pickles, and drink *lassi* (sweet or salty variations on buttermilk/yogurt) or beer.

OTTOLENGHI £

www.ottolenghi.co.uk

Merely looking at the restaurant is sustaining; eating here around the communal tables is even better. The Mediterranean-influenced dishes are fresh, colourful and full of flavour. Favourites include roast chicken with chilli and basil and roasted sweet potato with pecan and maple syrup. The restaurant is opposite the Almeida Theatre.

🔲 Off map ✉ 287 Upper Street, N1 ☎ 020 7288 1454 🕐 Mon–Sat 8am–11pm, Sun 9am–7pm 🚇 Angel, Highbury & Islington

OXO TOWER BAR, BRASSERIE & RESTAURANT ££–£££

www.harveynichols.com

Look out over London while eating, drinking or snacking on good British and pan-Asian food. There are plenty of outdoor tables; reservations are essential.

🔲 M6 ✉ 8th Floor, Oxo Tower Wharf, Barge House Street, SE1 ☎ 020 7803 3888 🕐 Mon–Fri 12–2.30, 6–11, Sat 12–2.30, 5.30–11, Sun 12–3, 6.30–10 🚇 Blackfriars

EAT

PAUL £

www.paul-uk.com

This stunning patisserie is a branch of its French mother founded in 1889. Sample divine hot chocolate and pastries. There are more than 20 other branches across London.

🚇 K5 ✉ 29 Bedford Street, WC2 ☎ 020 7836 3304 🕐 Mon–Fri 7.30am–9pm, Sat 9–9, Sun 9–8 🚇 Covent Garden

THE PEASANT £–££

www.thepeasant.co.uk

Expect a warm welcome at this classy north London gastropub. Classic and modern British food is served in the bar, with more sophisticated flavours on offer in the upstairs restaurant.

🚇 N3 ✉ 240 St. John Street, EC1 ☎ 020 7336 7726 🕐 Pub: Mon–Fri 12–11, Sat 6pm–11pm, Sun 12–10.30. Restaurant: Mon–Fri 12–3, 6–11, Sat 6pm–11pm, Sun 12–3 🚇 Farringdon

PORTRAIT RESTAURANT ££

www.searcys.co.uk

In this restaurant at the National Portrait Gallery every table benefits from the fine view. Try the salmon with a champagne cream sauce for a summer lunch. Reservations here are essential.

🚇 J5 ✉ National Portrait Gallery, St. Martin's Place, WC2 ☎ 020 7312 2490 🕐 Sun–Wed 10–5, Thu–Sat 10–8.15 🚇 Leicester Square, Charing Cross

PROVIDORES & TAPA ROOM ££

www.theprovidores.co.uk

Enjoy imaginative dishes and New Zealand wines at this café, wine bar and fine dining restaurant.

🚇 F3 ✉ 109 Marylebone High Street, W1 ☎ 020 7935 6175 🕐 Mon–Fri 9am–10.30pm, Sat 10am–10.30pm, Sun 10–10 🚇 Baker Street

RASA SAMUDRA £

www.rasarestaurants.com

One of several Rasa restaurants in the capital, Rasa Samudra serves inspired cooking from Kerala in southwest India, with seafood and vegetarian dishes as specialities.

🚇 H3 ✉ 6 Dering Street, W1 ☎ 020 7637 0222 🕐 Mon–Sat 12–3, 6–11, Sun 6–11 🚇 Goodge Street

RHODES TWENTY FOUR £££

www.rhodes24.co.uk

Gary Rhodes provides the ulitmate City experience: fine British food and amazing City views.

🚇 Q4 ✉ 24th floor, Tower 42, Old Broad Street, EC2 ☎ 020 7877 7703 🕐 Mon–Fri 12–2.30, 6–9 🚇 Liverpool Street

ROYAL CHINA £

www.royalchinagroup.co.uk

Reserve a table or join the justifiably long lines for the best dim sum in town. There are four branches.

🚇 A5 ✉ 13 Queensway, W2 ☎ 020 7221 2535 🕐 Mon–Thu 12–11, Fri–Sat 12–11.30, Sun 11–10 🚇 Queensway

RULES ££

www.rules.co.uk

Rules, founded in 1798, serves good traditional English dishes in plush Edwardian rooms.

🚇 K5 ✉ 35 Maiden Lane, WC2 ☎ 020 7836 5314 🕐 Mon–Sat 12–11.45, Sun 12–10.45 🚇 Covent Garden

ST. JOHN ££

www.stjohnrestaurant.com

The robust dishes on offer range from rabbit to oxtail to serious puddings, which include such delights as lemon posset.

🔲 N3 ✉ 26 St. John Street, EC1 ☎ 020 3301 8069 🕐 Mon–Fri 12–3, Mon–Sat 6pm–11pm, Sun 1–4 🚇 Farringdon

THE SQUARE £££

www.squarerestaurant.com

Impressive modern French food from Philip Howard is matched by a chic but formal Mayfair interior.

🔲 G5 ✉ 6–10 Bruton Street, W1 ☎ 020 7495 7100 🕐 Mon–Fri 12–2.30, 6.30–10, Sat 6.30–10.30, Sun 6.30–9.30 🚇 Bond Street

TAMARIND ££

www.tamarindrestaurant.com

Focusing on traditional Mughal cuisine, cooked in tandoor ovens and delicately spiced, Alfred Prassad won the UK's first Michelin star for an Indian restaurant.

🔲 G6 ✉ 20 Queen Street, W1 ☎ 020 7629 3561 🕐 Mon–Fri 12–2.45, 5.30–11, Sat 5.30–11, Sun 12–2.45, 6–10.30 🚇 Green Park

TATE MODERN CAFÉ £

www.tate.org.uk

Take a break from the art to enjoy upscale café food and Thames views. (For a grander meal, book at the rooftop restaurant.)

🔲 N6 ✉ Tate Modern, SE1 ☎ 020 7887 8888 🕐 Sun–Thu 10–5.30, Fri 10–9.30, Sat 10–6 🚇 Blackfriars, Southwark

TOM AIKENS £££

www.tomaikens.co.uk

Enjoy delicious haute cuisine and superb service in a fresh, contemporary setting.

🔲 D9 ✉ 43 Elystan Street, SW3 ☎ 020 7584 2003 🕐 Mon–Fri 12–2.30, 6.45–11, Sat 6.45–11 🚇 South Kensington

VILLANDRY ££

www.villandry.com

Villandry delights with its simple but tasty specialities. There's a French delicatessen, bakery and bar, too.

🔲 G3 ✉ 170 Great Portland Street, W1 ☎ 020 7631 3131 🕐 Mon–Fri 8am–11pm, Sat 9am–10.30pm 🚇 Great Portland Street, Oxford Circus

WILD HONEY ££–£££

www.wildhoneyrestaurant.co.uk

Enjoy quality modern European cooking in a stylishly simple Mayfair setting. The set lunch and pre-theatre menus are good value.

🔲 G5 ✉ 12 St. George Street, W1 ☎ 020 7758 9160 🕐 Mon–Sat 12–2.30, 6–11, Sun 12–3, 6–10.30 🚇 Oxford Circus, Bond Street

THE WOLSELEY ££

www.thewolseley.com

The Grand Café tradition continues at the Wolseley in Piccadilly. Start the day in art deco grandeur, or relax over afternoon tea after visiting the Royal Academy.

🔲 H6 ✉ 160 Piccadilly, W1 ☎ 020 7499 6996 🕐 Mon–Fri 7am–midnight, Sat 8am–midnight, Sun 8am–11pm 🚇 Green Park, Piccadilly Circus

WORLD FOOD CAFÉ £

www.worldfoodcafenealsyard.co.uk

This Neal's Yard restaurant offers a fresh approach to vegetarian food, combining Indian, Mexican, Greek and Turkish influences.

🔲 K4 ✉ 14 Neal's Yard, WC2 ☎ 020 7379 0298 🕐 Mon–Fri 11.30–4.30, Sat 11.30–5 🚇 Covent Garden

EAT

Sleep

Ranging from luxurious and modern upmarket hotels to simple budget hotels, London has accommodation to suit everyone. In this section establishments are listed alphabetically.

Introduction

London has many excellent hotels but room rates are very high, and it is certainly worth searching for special offers. Weekend and winter rates are often less expensive.

Reservations

Many hotels will ask you to pre-pay your reservation, or confirm with a credit card, and will charge a fee if you cancel at short notice or fail to turn up. Most hotels have rooms of different sizes, so always ask if there is a choice. Small hotels and guesthouses in historic buildings may not have a lift (elevator).

Outside Central London

If you are prepared to take a slightly longer bus or Tube ride to reach the sights, staying in a residential suburb provides a less expensive alternative to a pricey city-centre hotel.

Budget Accommodation

Consider alternatives to hotels, such as renting an apartment, staying in a bed-and-breakfast (B&B) or staying with a London family (for online information visit www.bedandbreakfast. com, www.athomeinlondon.co.uk, www. thebedandbreakfastclub.co.uk or the tourist board's Visit London website). During student vacations, inexpensive accommodation is offered by London university halls of residence (see www.universityrooms.co.uk and www.ish. org.uk). Youth hostels are another option (www.yha.org).

NOISE LEVELS

As most of London's accommodation options are situated on busy streets, noise can be a problem. Some hotels have double glazing, but that can make rooms unbearably stuffy, especially since air-conditioning is not standard. If you value peace and quiet, look for hotels on side streets in residential areas; or request a room at the rear of or higher up in the building.

Top to bottom: The exclusive Claridge's Hotel; the grand entrance to The Dorchester; London's top hotels offer superb service; a room at the Grosvenor Hotel

Directory

South Bank

Budget
Premier Inn
Mid-Range
Southwark Rose

Fleet Street to the Tower

Budget
Travelodge
Mid-Range
Chamberlain
Zetter Rooms
Luxury
Andaz
Malmaison
The Rookery

Covent Garden to Regent's Park

Budget
Generator Hostel
Morgan
Mid-Range
Academy
Luxury
Charlotte Street Hotel
Covent Garden Hotel
Hazlitt's
One Aldwych

St. Martin's Lane
Savoy

Westminster and St. James's

Luxury
The Goring
The Ritz

Around Hyde Park

Budget
22 York Street
Easyhotel
Pavilion Hotel
Mid-Range
Aster House
Kensington House
The Leonard
Luxury
The Berkeley
Blakes
The Dorchester
The Halkin

Further Afield

Budget
Clink 261
Mid-Range
Portobello

Sleeping A–Z

PRICES

Prices are approximate and based on a double room for one night.

£££	Over £250
££	£150–£250
£	under £150

22 YORK STREET £

www.22yorkstreet.co.uk
This elegant five-storey Georgian town house close to Regent's Park has been transformed into a quality bed-and-breakfast.
➕ E3 ✉ 22 York Street, W1 ☎ 020 7224 2990 🚇 Baker Street

ACADEMY ££

www.theetoncollection.com
Convenient for the British Museum, this 49-room boutique hotel is set in five converted Georgian town houses.
➕ J3 ✉ 21 Gower Street, WC1 ☎ 020 7631 4115 🚇 Goodge Street

ANDAZ £££
www.london.liverpoolstreet.andaz.hyatt.com
Casual 21st-century luxury is the theme of this stylishly converted Victorian railway hotel.
➕ R3 ✉ 40 Liverpool Street, EC2 ☎ 020 7961 1234 Ⓜ Liverpool Street

ASTER HOUSE ££
www.asterhouse.com
Aster House stands with other chic B&Bs in a smart South Kensington stuccoed terrace, near the museums. You can enjoy the garden, palm-filled conservatory and power showers.
➕ C9 ✉ 3 Sumner Place, SW3 ☎ 020 7581 5888 Ⓜ South Kensington

THE BERKELEY £££
www.the-berkeley.co.uk
Guests at this luxury Knightsbridge hotel enjoy traditional elegance, plus famed service and food. Facilities include a spa, rooftop pool and two great restaurants.
➕ E7 ✉ Wilton Place, SW1 ☎ 020 7235 6000 Ⓜ Hyde Park Corner, Knightsbridge

BLAKES ££–£££
www.blakeshotels.com
Designer Anoushka Hempel has achieved sumptuous decadence in this South Kensington boutique

---

LOCATION

It is well worth perusing the London map to decide where you are likely to spend most of your time. Then select a hotel in that area or accessible to it by Underground on a direct line, so you avoid having to change trains. London is vast and it takes time to cross, particularly by bus and costly taxis. By paying a little more to be in the heart of the city, you will save on travel time and costs.

---

hotel. There are just 41 rooms, plus a restaurant and bar.
➕ Off map ✉ 33 Roland Gardens, SW7 ☎ 020 7370 6701 Ⓜ South Kensington, Gloucester Road

CHAMBERLAIN ££
www.fullershotels.com
Set in lavishly converted 20th-century offices in the City of London, this hotel has 64 comfortable bedrooms. There is a popular pub on the premises.
➕ S4 ✉ 130–135 Minories, EC3 ☎ 020 7680 1500 Ⓜ Fenchurch Street, Aldgate

CHARLOTTE STREET HOTEL £££
www.firmdale.com
Kit and Tim Kemp's boutique cocktail of comfort and fairy-tale Englishness has 52 rooms.
➕ H3 ✉ 15 Charlotte Street, W1 ☎ 020 7806 2000 Ⓜ Goodge Street

CLINK 261 £
www.ashleehouse.co.uk
This funky backpacker hostel, convenient for Eurostar departures from London St. Pancras, has 170 beds in 33 rooms.
➕ K1 ✉ 261–265 Gray's Inn Road, WC1 ☎ 020 7833 9400 Ⓜ King's Cross

COVENT GARDEN HOTEL £££
www.firmdale.com
Another of Kit Kemp's stylish boutique hotels, this one attracts film stars who enjoy its 58 traditional yet contemporary British rooms, bathrooms and library.
➕ J4 ✉ 10 Monmouth Street, WC2 ☎ 020 7806 1000 Ⓜ Leicester Square

THE DORCHESTER £££
www.thedorchester.com
The Dorchester is one of London's finest hotels. Deliciously art deco,

it is a London landmark from its grand entrance and piano bar to the Oliver Messel suite. The hotel's some 250 bedrooms have huge, luxury bathrooms.

F6 ⊠ Park Lane, W1 ☎ 020 7629 8888 ⊜ Green Park, Hyde Park Corner

EASYHOTEL £

www.easyhotel.com

Easyhotel is inexpensive but basic in the extreme; few of the 34 rooms have windows.

A8 ⊠ 14 Lexham Gardens, W8 ☎ Reserve by website only ⊜ Earl's Court, Gloucester Road

GENERATOR HOSTEL £

www.generatorhostels.com

This industrial-style building offers 870 guests bunk-bedded rooms, excellent facilities and a party atmosphere. 217 rooms.

K2 ⊠ 37 Tavistock Place, WC1 ☎ 020 7388 7666 ⊜ Russell Square

THE GORING £££

www.thegoring.com

High standards of old-fashioned hospitality and service make this

splendid hotel memorable. Owned by the Goring family for over a century, the hotel has 74 classic rooms.

G8 ⊠ Beeston Place, Grosvenor Gardens, SW1 ☎ 020 7396 9000 ⊜ Victoria

THE HALKIN £££

www.halkin.como.bz

Opened 20 years ago, central London's first boutique hotel blends western and Asian aesthetics. It has 41 rooms and a good Thai restaurant.

F7 ⊠ 4 Halkin Street, SW1 ☎ 020 7333 1000 ⊜ Hyde Park Corner

SLEEP

The Dorchester, one of the capital's finest hotels

The Savoy, a byword for luxury

HAZLITT'S £££

www.hazlittshotel.com

The 23-room Hazlitt's offers near-perfect period decoration in three 18th-century houses, plus a superb location for theatres.

➕ J4 ✉ 6 Frith Street, W1 ☎ 020 7434 1771 🚇 Tottenham Court Road

KENSINGTON HOUSE ££

www.kenhouse.com

This beautifully restored 19th-century property provides contemporary accommodation in the heart of Kensington. The 41 bedrooms are light and stylish.

➕ A7 ✉ 15–16 Prince of Wales Terrace, W8 ☎ 020 7937 2345 🚇 High Street Kensington

THE LEONARD ££–£££

www.theleonard.com

A discreet, small hotel, near busy Oxford Street, the Leonard has 28 comfortable bedrooms and luxury apartments.

➕ E4 ✉ 15 Seymour Street, W1 ☎ 020 7935 2010 🚇 Marble Arch

MALMAISON £££

www.malmaison.com

Relax in the stylish, contemporary rooms at this hotel with a brasserie and bar in trendy Clerkenwell.

➕ N3 ✉ 18 Charterhouse Square, EC1 ☎ 020 7012 3700 🚇 Farringdon

MORGAN £

www.morganhotel.co.uk

Family-run, friendly and well-located, the Morgan has just 20 rooms, so book ahead.

➕ J3 ✉ 24 Bloomsbury Street, WC1 ☎ 020 7636 3735 🚇 Tottenham Court Road

ONE ALDWYCH £££

www.onealdwych.com

A stylish, 105-room contemporary hotel in an Edwardian building, One Aldwych epitomizes restrained luxury.

➕ L5 ✉ 1 Aldwych, WC2 ☎ 020 7300 1000 🚇 Covent Garden, Temple

PAVILION HOTEL £

www.pavilionhoteluk.com

The plain facade at the 30-room Pavilion Hotel belies the witty fantasy decor inside.

➕ C4 ✉ 34–36 Sussex Gardens, W2 ☎ 020 7262 0905 🚇 Paddington

PORTOBELLO ££

www.portobello-hotel.co.uk

A romantic retreat with 24 exotic, sumptuous rooms, the hotel is close to the antiques shops of Portobello Road.

🛏 Off map ✉ 22 Stanley Gardens, W11
☎ 020 7727 2777 🚇 Notting Hill Gate

PREMIER INN £

www.premierinn.com

In County Hall, opposite the Houses of Parliament, this 313-room hotel is the star London location of the no-frills chain.

🛏 L7 ✉ County Hall, Belvedere Road, SE1
☎ 0871 527 8648 🚇 Waterloo

THE RITZ £££

www.theritzlondon.com

Guests enjoy sumptuous luxury, with traditional style, gilt decor and the great first-floor promenade to London's most beautiful dining room, overlooking Green Park.

🛏 G6 ✉ 150 Piccadilly, W1 ☎ 020 7493 8181 🚇 Green Park

THE ROOKERY £££

www.rookeryhotel.co.uk

Enjoy discreet comforts in this atmospheric 33-room hotel, enhanced with antiques, open fires and Victorian bathrooms.

🛏 N3 ✉ Cowcross Street, EC1 ☎ 020 7336 0931 🚇 Farringdon

ST. MARTIN'S LANE £££

www.stmartinslane.com

Ian Schrager and Philippe Starck's fabulous 204-room hotel in Covent Garden is a celebration of theatrical minimalism.

🛏 J5 ✉ St. Martin's Lane, WC2 ☎ 020 7300 5500 🚇 Covent Garden, Leicester Square

SAVOY £££

www.savoygroup.com

A top-to-toe refurbishment has brought this grand London hotel firmly into the 21st century.

🛏 L5 ✉ Strand, WC2 ☎ 020 7836 4343 🚇 Covent Garden

SOUTHWARK ROSE ££

www.all-seasons-hotels.com

With 84 contemporary rooms, this hotel is close to Tate Modern and, via the Millennium Bridge, the rest of the city centre. It has notable family suites with kitchenettes.

🛏 P6 ✉ 43–47 Southwark Bridge Road, SE1 ☎ 020 7015 1480 🚇 London Bridge

TRAVELODGE £

www.travelodge.co.uk

Part of the no-frills chain of modern hotels, this is a good budget choice, particularly for families.

🛏 S5 ✉ 1 Goodmans Yard, Lloyds Court Business Centre, E1 ☎ 0871 984 6388 🚇 Tower Hill

ZETTER ROOMS ££

www.thezetter.com

A hip contemporary hotel in Clerkenwell, with restaurant and bar to match, the Zetter has 59 rooms. There are great views of the City from the rooftop suites.

🛏 N2 ✉ St. John's Square, 86–88 Clerkenwell Road, EC1 ☎ 020 7324 4444 🚇 Farringdon

SLEEP

BARGAIN LUXURY

To be pampered amid sumptuous surroundings may be an essential part of your trip. London's most luxurious hotels have been built with no expense spared. Hotel prices are generally very high, but quality rooms can be had for bargain prices. It's always worth asking when you make your reservation whether any special deals are available. Most deluxe and mid-range hotels offer weekend deals throughout the year.

THAMES PATH

MPERIAL WAR MUSEUM

LONDON AQUARIUM

THAMES PATH
Hungerford Bridge

ST. THOMAS'S HOSPIT
(Florence Nightingale Mus

WHITEHALL

EMBANKMENT

WESTMINSTER

Need to Know

This section takes you through all the practical aspects of your trip to make it run more smoothly and to give you confidence before you go and while you are there.

NEED TO KNOW

Planning Ahead

WHEN TO GO

The tourist season is year-round, and most attractions remain open all year. Peak season is from June to September, when you should arrive with a hotel reservation and theatre tickets. The quietest months are February, March, October and November, when hotels may give a discount.

TIME

GMT (Greenwich Mean Time) is standard. BST (British Summer Time) is 1 hour ahead (late Mar–late Oct).

TEMPERATURE

JAN	FEB	MAR	APR	MAY	JUN	JUL	AUG	SEP	OCT	NOV	DEC
42°F	45°F	50°F	55°F	63°F	68°F	72°F	72°F	66°F	57°F	50°F	45°F
6°C	7°C	10°C	13°C	17°C	20°C	22°C	22°C	19°C	14°C	10°C	7°C

Spring (March to May) has a mixture of sunshine and showers, although winter often encroaches on it.

Summer (June to August) can be unpredictable, with clear skies and hot days interspersed with rain, sultry greyness or thunderstorms.

Autumn (September to November) has clear skies that can feel almost summery. Real autumn starts in October, and colder weather sets in during November.

Winter (December to February) is generally fairly cold, and snow has been disruptive in recent years.

WHAT'S ON

January *Sales:* Shopping bargains at stores all over the city.

February *Chinese New Year:* Dragon dances and fireworks in Soho.

March *Chelsea Antiques Fair:* Chelsea Old Town Hall.

April *Oxford and Cambridge Boat Race* (1st Sat): This famous annual race takes place on the Thames from Putney to Mortlake.

London Marathon: The world's biggest running race.

May *Chelsea Flower Show* (end of May): One of the world's best takes place at the Royal Hospital, Chelsea.

June *Trooping the Colour* (2nd Sat): The 'Colours' (flags) are trooped before the Queen on Horseguards Parade, Whitehall.

Wimbledon (Jun/Jul): The world's leading grass tennis tournament.

July *Promenade Concerts* (Jul–Aug): Nightly world-class classical concerts in the Albert Hall.

August *Notting Hill Carnival* (last Sun and Bank Holiday Monday): Europe's biggest carnival.

September *Mayor's Thames Festival:* London's largest outdoor arts festival, a free weekend extravaganza on and around the river.

October *Pearly Kings and Queens* (1st Sun): Service at St. Martin-in-the-Fields.

BFI London Film Festival.

November *Bonfire Night* (5 Nov): Fires and fireworks commemorate the failed Gunpowder Plot of 1605.

State Opening of Parliament: Royal procession from Buckingham Palace to the Houses of Parliament.

December *Christmas music* (all month): Christmas music fills London's churches.

USEFUL WEBSITES

www.visitlondon.com
London's official site is up-to-date and comprehensive with ideas for museums, theatre and restaurants, and sections for children and visitors with disabilities. It offers discounts, too.

www.royalparks.gov.uk
From Greenwich Park to Green Park, all eight of London's Royal Parks are detailed here, with information on special events and activities for children.

www.tfl.gov.uk
London Transport's official site gives ideas for what to see and do, ticket information for the Underground, buses, DLR and river services. It also has a WAP-enabled journey planner.

www.royal.gov.uk
The official site of the British royal family, with history, royal residences, who's doing what today and a monthly online magazine.

www.bhrconline.com
The British Hotel Reservation Centre website takes bookings, from bed-and-breakfasts to grand hotels. Special discounts are included.

www.londontown.com
This comprehensive site covers what's on, what's new, attractions, events, theatres, sightseeing ideas, traditions, nightlife, shopping, markets and general advice.

www.hrp.org.uk
This site is dedicated to London's five great historic palaces, from the Tower of London to Hampton Court.

www.officiallondontheatre.co.uk
The Society of London Theatre's official site, with all the latest theatre news, together with comprehensive interviews with stars, performance details and theatre access for people with disabilities.

PRIME TRAVEL SITES

www.nationaltrust.org.uk
This independent organization owns and maintains many buildings and extensive lands, some of them in and around London.

www.english-heritage.org.uk/London
English Heritage are responsible for many historic sites and buildings—many are in London.

www.fodors.com
A complete travel-planning site. You can research prices and weather; book air tickets, cars and rooms; pose questions (and get answers) from fellow travellers; and find links to other sites.

INTERNET CAFÉS

● **easyInternetcafé**
(easyEverything.com): The international chain started in London is open seven days a week and has branches throughout the city. The one at 160–166 Kensington High Street has almost 400 terminals.

● All of the capital's public libraries have internet facilities. WiFi is available at Starbucks cafés, major train stations and airports. Most hotels have modem plug-in-points (data ports) or WiFi in each room.

Getting There

NEED TO KNOW

AIRPORT TIP

Savvy Londoners use the Heathrow Connect service (www.heathrowconnect.com) to Paddington station. Two trains an hour operate on this stopping service; the journey time is around 25 minutes and the cost is under half that of the express fares.

TRAINS

● For all information
☎ 08457 484950;
www.nationalrail.co.uk
● Purchase tickets at the railway station or on online at www.thetrainline.com.
● All major London train stations are on Tube lines.
● There are eight major London train stations; sometimes a town is served by more than one (e.g., Paddington and Waterloo both serve Windsor).
● Train fares are high but there are lots of cheap deals if you book in advance and can be flexible about the time you travel.

AIRPORTS

Heathrow and Gatwick are the principal airports serving the city. However, Stansted, Luton and London City are becoming increasingly busy with traffic from Continental Europe. There are train links to the continent via Lille and Paris and road links to Channel ports.

60km (40 miles)

Luton Airport
Bus 1hr 30min
Train 25min

Stansted Airport
Bus 1hr 40min
Train 40min

London City Airport
Bus 25–40min
DLR/Underground 25min

Heathrow Airport
Bus approx 1hr
Train approx 15min
Underground 1hr

Gatwick Airport
Bus 1hr 30min–2hr 45 min
Train 30min

FROM HEATHROW

Heathrow (tel 0870 000 0123; www. heathrow airport.com) has five terminals, some 24km (15 miles) west of central London; all are well served by public transport. The Underground Piccadilly line runs from 5am–11.40pm (6am–11.20pm Sunday); and takes about an hour. The Heathrow Express (tel 0845 600 1515; www.heathrowexpress. com), a high-speed rail link to Paddington station, runs from 5.10am–11.40pm every 15 minutes. Ticket prices are high for the 15-minute journey. National Express (tel 08717 818181) buses run from 5.30am–9.40pm to Victoria Coach Station, journey time around one hour. Taxis wait outside any terminal; the trip takes under an hour, depending on the traffic, and costs around £70 (www.heathrowtaxis.org).

FROM GATWICK

Gatwick airport (tel 0844 335 1802; www. gatwickairport.com) is 48km (30 miles) south of the heart of the city. The best way to reach London is by train: The Gatwick Express (tel 0845 850 1530; www.gatwickexpress. com) train leaves for Victoria Station every

15 minutes, (5am–1am) and takes 30 minutes. Southern runs slightly slower but cheaper services; and First Capital Connect's Thameslink leads direct to the City and King's Cross/St. Pancras International. Taxis cost more than £100.

FROM STANSTED

Stansted airport (tel 0844 335 1803; www. stanstedairport.com) is 56km (35 miles) northeast of central London. The Stansted Express (tel 0845 850 0150; www. stanstedexpress.com) to Liverpool Street Station takes around 40 minutes. Several bus/ coach operators run services to Liverpool Street and Victoria stations. Journey time is up to 1 hour 40 minutes. A taxi costs from £100.

FROM LUTON AIRPORT

Luton airport (tel 01582 405 100; www.london-luton.co.uk) is 53km (33 miles) north of London. There are bus links to Victoria Coach Station, taking around 1 hour 30 minutes, and East Midlands and Thameslink trains to St. Pancras International, taking from 25 minutes. Taxis cost about £80.

FROM LONDON CITY AIRPORT

City Airport (tel 020 7646 0088; www.londoncityairport.com) is at Royal Albert Docks, 9 miles (14km) east of central London. Trains from London City Airport feed into the Underground (Tube) system. Taxis wait outside the terminal and cost around £35.

THE CHANNEL TUNNEL

Eurostar train services (tel 08432 186186; www.eurostar.com) connect Britain to Continental Europe, and are a great way of arriving in London, plus taking trips out to Paris, Brussels and elsewhere. Book ahead for cheap deals. Trains use St. Pancras International terminal, close to King's Cross. Eurotunnel (tel 08433 353535; www.eurotunnel.com) is for vehicles only. Fares are lower if you reserve ahead.

BY COACH

If you travel to London by long-distance coach you will probably arrive at Victoria Coach Station (VCS) on Buckingham Palace Road, near Victoria main train station. The coach station is a few minutes' walk from the Underground station, which is on the Victoria, District and Circle lines. Alternatively, there is a taxi rank immediately outside VCS.

LOST/STOLEN PROPERTY

The most seasoned traveller occasionally leaves something behind—airlines find forgotten computers almost daily.

● Contact the place where you think you left it or saw it last.

● Report the loss to a police station and get a copy of the report form for your insurance claim.

● If you lose a passport, report it to the police and your embassy. Provided you have photocopies of the key pages, it should not be difficult to replace.

● Contact for London Transport and taxi lost property ☎ 0845 330 9882; www.tfl.gov.uk

Getting Around

DRIVING TIP

Driving in London is slow, parking is expensive and fines are high. Congestion charges operate from Monday to Friday, 7am–6pm, costing £10 a day. Do not drive in London unless you have to: use public transport.

VISITORS WITH DISABILITIES

London is steadily improving its facilities for visitors with disabilities, from shops and theatres to hotels and museums. The Government is introducing free admission for those with disabilities. Newer attractions such as Tate Modern and the London Eye are better equipped than ancient buildings such as Westminster Abbey. Check out the London Tourist Board's comprehensive website www.visitlondon.com and guide books, such as *Access in London* (published by Access Project PHSP ✉ 39 Bradley Gardens, W13; www. accessinlondon.org). Also consult Artsline (www. artsline.org.uk), Can Be Done (www.canbedone.co.uk) and Dial (www.dialuk.info). William Forrester, a lecturer and wheelchair user, leads tailor-made tours in the city (☎ 01483 575401).

Underground trains (known as the Tube) and buses run from around 5.30am to just after midnight, when service is via a night bus. The transport system is divided into zones (clearly indicated on transport maps) and you must have a ticket valid for the zone you are in. If you anticipate making more than one journey, buy a Travelcard (▷ 167), which allows unlimited use of the Underground, buses and Docklands Light Railway (DLR) services. Travel information tel 0843 222 1234; www.tfl.gov.uk.

THE UNDERGROUND (TUBE)

Twelve colour-coded lines link almost 300 stations. Use a travel pass or buy a ticket from a machine or ticket booth; keep the ticket until the end of the journey. The system includes the Docklands Light Railway (DLR).

BUSES

Plan your journey using the latest copy of the Central London bus guide available at London Transport information centres (▷ 167) or at www.tfl.gov.uk. A flat cash fare applies across London. Tickets must be bought from a machine at the bus stop. A bus stop is indicated by a red sign on a metal pole displaying diagrams of each route it serves.

From 2012, new red double-decker buses will be introduced, combining cutting-edge design and technology with nostalgia for the old Routemaster buses.

TAXIS

Taxis that are available for rental illuminate a yellow 'For Hire' sign on the roof. Hold out your hand to hail them beside the road. Drivers of official cabs will know the city well. They are obliged to follow the shortest route unless an alternative is agreed beforehand. A 'black cab' (now often not black but a bright colour) is licensed for up to five passengers. Meter charges increase in the evenings and at weekends. Avoid minicabs if you can as they may have no meter and possibly inadequate

insurance. Call a black cab via Radio Taxis
tel 020 7272 0272; www.radiotaxis.co.uk.

TRAVEL INFORMATION CENTRES
These sell travel passes and provide Tube and
train maps, bus route maps and information
on cheap tickets. They are open daily at the
following stations: Heathrow terminals 1, 2
and 3, Liverpool Street, Victoria, Euston, King's
Cross and Piccadilly Circus. Transport for
London service, tel 0843 222 1234.

TRAVEL PASSES
Travelcards, valid after 9.30am (pay a sur-
charge to use earlier), for unlimited travel by
Tube, railway, Docklands Light Railway and
buses, are sold at travel information centres,
railway and Tube stations, and some shops.
They cover travel for one day or seven days.

   Oyster prepay Smartcards are valid for use
on the Underground, DLR, bus, Thameslink
and some national rail networks. Single fares
are much cheaper with Oyster than cash and
the cards can be topped up with more credit.

LONDON PASS
This is a pass to more than 50 top attractions
as well as an option to travel on buses, the
Tube and trains. The aim of the pass is to
enable you to beat the crowds lining up at
selected major attractions. The pass is valid for
either one, two, three or six days—multi-day
passes must be used on consecutive days. It
offers discounts on restaurants and leisure
activities. See www.londonpass.com for details.

BOATING AND BIKING
Thames Clippers (www.thamesclippers.com)
runs a commuter, leisure and sightseeing
service aboard high-speed catamarans.

   London Cycling Campaign (www.lcc.org.uk)
and the London Cycle Network (www.london
cyclenetwork.org.uk) advise on all aspects of
biking in the capital. Visitors can rent a
bicycle from one of the Barclays Cycle Hire
project docking stations scattered across
central and east London (www.tfl.gov.uk).

TIPS
● London is huge. It may
take more than an hour to
reach your destination, so
allow plenty of time—and
plan your day to avoid criss-
crossing the city.
● Buy a travelcard, which is
valid for the entire transport
network. Select the appropriate pass for the areas you
will visit. Many people find
the Zones 1 and 2 range is
adequate; pay a supplement
when you go outside it.
● Use common sense when
travelling alone at night, but
there is no need to be unduly
concerned.
● Do not smoke on any
public transport—it is
banned.

FUN TOURS
There are many quirky ways
to see London. Below are
some ideas:
● London Walks ☎ 020
7624 3978; www.walks.com.
● Open House Architecture
☎ 020 7383 2131;
www.open-city.org.uk.
● Cabair Helicopters
☎ 020 8953 4411;
www.cabairhelicopters.com.
● By water (▷ 56–57).
● London Duck Tours
☎ 020 7928 3132;
www.londonducktours.co.uk.

Essential Facts

VISAS AND TRAVEL INSURANCE

Check visa and passport requirements before travelling, see www.fco.gov.uk or ukinusa.fco.gov.uk. EU citizens are covered for medical expenses with an EHIC card; insurance to cover illness and theft is still strongly advised. Visitors from outside the EU should check their insurance coverage and if necessary, buy a supplementary policy.

MONEY

Try to arrive at the airport or train station with some British coins or some £10 or £5 notes. If you travel to your hotel by Tube, the self-service machines accept both money and credit cards.

CREDIT CARDS

● Credit cards are widely accepted; Visa and MasterCard are the most popular, followed by AmericanExpress, Diners Club and JCB. Credit cards can also be used for withdrawing cash from ATMs at any bank displaying the appropriate sign.
● If your credit cards are lost, report each one immediately to the relevant company and the police; also call your bank. To discover your credit card company's local 24-hour emergency number, go to www.ukphonebook.co.uk; it's free but you have to register.

ELECTRICITY

● Standard supply is 240V. Motor-driven equipment needs a specific frequency; in the UK it is 50 cycles per second (kHz).

EMERGENCY TELEPHONE NUMBERS

● For police, fire or ambulance, tel 999 from any telephone, free of charge. The call goes directly to the emergency services. Tell the operator which street you are on and the nearest landmark, intersection or house number; stay by the telephone until help arrives.

MEDICAL TREATMENT

● EU nationals and citizens of some other countries with special arrangements (Australia and New Zealand) may receive free National Health Service (NHS) medical treatment if they have the correct documentation (an EHIC card for EU visitors).
● All other visitors have to pay.
● If you need an ambulance tel 999 on any telephone, free of charge, or 112 from most mobiles/cellphones.
● NHS hospitals with 24-hour emergency departments include: University College Hospital, Gower Street (entrance in Grafton Way), WC1, tel 0845 155 5000; Chelsea and Westminster Hospital, 369 Fulham Road, SW10, tel 020 8746 8000.
● Private hospitals, with no emergency unit, include the Cromwell Hospital, 162–174 Cromwell Road, SW5, tel 020 7460 2000.
● Great Chapel Street Medical Centre, 13 Great Chapel Street, W1, tel 020 7437 9360, is an NHS clinic open to all, but visitors from countries without the NHS reciprocal agreement must pay.
● NHS Direct: tel 0845 4647.
● Dental advice: tel 0845 063 1188, Mon–Fri 9–5.
● Eye specialist: Moorfields Eye Hospital, City Road, EC1, tel 020 7253 3411; City Road, EC1, tel 020 7253 3411; Vision Express, 263–265 Oxford Street, W1, tel 020 7409 7880; 020 7495 8209 (opticians and on-site

workshop for glasses and contact lenses).
● For homeopathic pharmacies, practitioners and advice: the British Homeopathic Association, tel 01582 408675; www.britishhomeopathic.org

MEDICINES
● Many drugs cannot be bought over the counter. For an NHS prescription, you pay a modest flat rate; if a private doctor prescribes, you pay the full cost. To claim charges back on insurance, keep receipts. Chemists that keep longer hours include: Bliss Chemist, 5 Marble Arch, W1, tel 020 7723 6116, daily 9am–midnight; Boots Midnight Pharmacy, 44–6 Regent Street, Piccadilly Circus, W1, tel 020 7734 6126, Mon–Fri 8am–midnight, Sat 9am–midnight, Sun 12–6.

OPENING HOURS
● Major attractions: seven days a week; some open late certain days of each week.
● Shops: generally Mon–Sat 9.30/10am–6pm; department stores until 8 or even 10pm (Selfridges, Oxford Street). Many shops open Sun 12–5/6pm; department stores have 'browsing time' before the tills open from 11.30am. Late-night shopping (until 8pm) is on Thu in the West End and Wed in Knightsbridge.
● Banks: Mon–Fri 9.30–5; a few remain open later or open on Sat mornings. *Bureaux de change* generally have longer opening hours. ATMs are abundant.
● Post offices: usually Mon–Fri 9–5.30, Sat 9–12.30.

NEWSPAPERS AND MAGAZINES

Newspapers include the *Financial Times*, *The Daily Telegraph*, *The Independent*, *The Guardian*, *The Daily Mail* and *The Times*, Sunday papers include *The Sunday Times*, *Sunday Telegraph*, *The Observer* and *Independent on Sunday*. Free papers (Mon–Fri) are *Metro* and *London Evening Standard*, which is strong on entertainment and nightlife (www.thisislondon.co.uk). *Time Out* (www.timeout.com), published weekly on Wed), lists almost everything going.

TIPPING

Many restaurants add a 12.5 per cent service charge. For taxis, hairdressers and other services, 10 per cent is acceptable. Tips are not usual in theatres, cinemas or concert halls, or in pubs or bars (unless there is table service).

NEED TO KNOW

EMBASSIES

Australian High Commission	✉ Australia House, Strand, WC2 ☎ 020 7379 4334; www.australia.org.uk
Canadian High Commission	✉ 1 Grosvenor Square, W1 ☎ 020 7358 6600; www.unitedkingdom.gc.ca
New Zealand High Commission	✉ New Zealand House, 80 Haymarket, SW1 ☎ 020 7930 8422; www.nzembassy.com
Embassy of the US	✉ 24 Grosvenor Square, W1 ☎ 020 7499 9000; http://londonusembassy.gov

Stamps are sold at post offices and some newsagents and shops. Trafalgar Square Post Office stays open late: ✉ William IV Street, WC2 🕐 Mon–Fri 8.30–6.30, Sat 9–5.30. Letter boxes are red.

TELEVISION

● Excluding satellite, cable and digital, there are five main national terrestrial channels in Britain: BBC1, BBC2, ITV1, Channel 4 and Channel 5. The BBC is funded by a licence fee and there is no advertising on any BBC channels.

● Relatively few homes in Britain have cable, although it is increasing. With analogue signals being phased out, digital terrestrial and digital satellite television services can be received in all homes, with a large number of channels and wide variety of content, available either free or through subscription. Programmes can also be viewed on the internet and 3G mobile/cell phones.

STUDENTS

Holders of an International Student Identity Card will be able to obtain some good concessions on travel and entrance fees.

PUBLIC HOLIDAYS

● 1 Jan; Good Fri; Easter Mon; May Day (first Mon in May); last Mon in May; last Mon in Aug; 25 Dec; 26 Dec.
● Almost all attractions and shops close Christmas Day; many close 24 Dec, 1 Jan and Good Fri as well. Some shops, restaurants and attractions remain open throughout, but check.

SENSIBLE PRECAUTIONS

● Keep valuables in a hotel or bank safe box.
● Note all passport, ticket and credit card numbers, and keep separately. Carry photo-copies of the key pages of your passport.
● Make sure that bags are fully closed and keep them in sight at all times—do not put them on the floor or over the back of a chair.
● At night, try not to travel alone; if you must, either prebook a taxi (not a mini-cab) or keep to well-lit streets and use a bus or Tube train where there are other people.

PHONES

● London numbers (now 8 digits) are pre-fixed with the code 020 when dialling from outside the city. To call London from abroad, dial the country code 44, then just 20, then the 8 digit number.
● Public phones accept coins, phonecards and credit cards.
● For the operator tel 100. For the interna-tional operator or to reverse charges tel 155.
● Directory enquiries: there are many options; tel 0800 953 0720 for details and prices.
● To make international calls from the UK, dial 00, then the country code (1 for the US).
● Beware of high charges on numbers pre-fixed 08 or 09 (0800 is free, 0845 and 0843 inexpensive).
● Before departure, consult with your cell/mobile phone provider on coverage and rates.

TOURIST INFORMATION
● **London Information Centre**
Leicester Square, W1, tel 020 7292 2333; www.londontown.com; daily 8am–midnight, Leicester Square.

Books and Films

London's vitality, variety, glamour and squalor have always provided rich pickings for writers and film makers.

London: The Biography (2000) and *Thames: Secret River* (2007) by historian Peter Ackroyd are essential background reading for visitors to the city. For fans of historical fiction, C.J. Sansom's Matthew Shardlake series (2003–2010) brilliantly evokes London at the time of Henry VIII.

Muriel Spark used life in post-war Kensington as the setting for her novella *The Girls of Slender Means* (1963); in *A Severed Head* (1961), Iris Murdoch foresaw the sexual revolution and Swinging London of the 1960s, while Doris Lessing had her character Martha Quest experience the social changes of the Cold War years in her controversial *The Four-Gated City* (1969). The amusing *Bridget Jones's Diary* (1997) by Helen Fielding defined a generation of 30-something women living in London in the late 1990s.

With his autobiographical *Fever Pitch* (1992) and fictional *About a Boy* (1998), Nick Hornby took a different angle on youthful London, as did Hanif Kureishi with his mixed-race teenage protagonist Karim in *The Buddha of Suburbia* (1990).

At the turn of the 21st century, multi-national, multi-denominational London was being explored by writers such as Zadie Smith in *White Teeth* (2001), Monica Ali in *Brick Lane* (2001) and Andrea Levy, who delved into migration from the Caribbean in the excellent *Small Island* (2004).

Several of these more recent novels have made their way onto the big screen, but for many people the most iconic movies are Michael Caine's lad-about-town *Alfie* (1966), the crime comedy *A Fish Called Wanda* (1988), the two *Bridget Jones* films (2001, 2004) and writer/director Richard Curtis's romantic comedies *Four Weddings and a Funeral* (1994), *Notting Hill* (1999) and *Love Actually* (2003), with the oh-so-English Hugh Grant in their leading roles.

LONDON CLASSICS

Perhaps the most famous book about London is *The Diary of Samuel Pepys*, in which the observer, Pepys, recorded events from 1600 to 1669. Many of Charles Dickens' novels have London settings, including *Oliver Twist* (1837), *The Old Curiosity Shop* (1840), *Bleak House* (1853) and *Little Dorrit* (1857). In 1887, Sir Arthur Conan Doyle introduced his character Sherlock Holmes in the novel *A Study in Scarlet*. The legendary fictional detective lived at 221b Baker Street, W1. In William Thackeray's *Vanity Fair* (1847), Becky Sharp begins her adventures in Russell Square. Humorist P.G. Wodehouse, creator of the eccentric Jeeves and Wooster, based his Drones Club on several London gentlemen's clubs of the time (1920s).

Index

The Automobile Association would like to thank the following photographers, companies and picture libraries for their assistance in the preparation of this book.

Abbreviations for the picture credits are as follows – (t) top; (b) bottom; (c) centre; (l) left; (r) right; (AA) AA World Travel Library.

2i AA/S Montgomery; **2ii** AA/N Setchfield; **2iii** AA/J Tims; **2iv** AA/S Montgomery; **2v** AA/J Tims; **3i–3ii** AA/J Tims; **3iii** AA/R Mort; **3iv** AA/S Montgomery; **4tl** AA/S Montgomery; **5** AA/J Tims; **6/7t** Kathy deWitt/Alamy; **6ct** Julio Etchart/Alamy; **6cb** Julio Etchart/Alamy; **7ct** Julio Etchart/Alamy; **7cb** Courtesy Arup; **6/7b** Courtesy Transport for London; **8/9t** AA/S Montgomery; **8/9ct** AA/N Setchfield; **8cb** AA/J Tims; **8/9b** AA/N Setchfield; **9ct** AA/J Tims; **9cb** AA/J Tims; **10bl** AA/J Tims; **10br** The Art Archive/Alamy; **11bl** Mary Evans Picture Library/Alamy; **11br** AA/J Tims; **12** AA/N Setchfield; **14l** AA/J Tims; **14tr** AA/S Montgomery; **14/15c** AA/J Tims; **15tl** AA/J Tims; **16** AA/J Tims; **17tl** AA/N Setchfield; **17tr** AA/J Tims; **17c** AA/J Tims; **18/19** AA/J Tims; **19tc** AA/S Montgomery; **19tr** Courtesy Royal Collection 2011, Her Majesty Queen Elizabeth II/Derry Moore; **19c** Monica Wells/TTL; **20** AA/N Setchfield; **21tl** AA/J Tims; **21cl** AA/S and O Mathews; **21c** AA/N Setchfield; **21tr** Courtesy Cutty Sark Trust; **22/23t–22/23c** AA/J Tims; **23c** AA/J Tims; **23tr** AA/J Tims; **24** London Stills; **25tl** AA/J Tims; **25tr** AA/S Montgomery; **25cl** London Stills; **25cr** AA/J Tims; **26** Courtesy Harvey Nichols; **27tl** Courtesy Swarovski/Yellow Door; **27tr** Travelshots.com/Alamy; **27cl** Courtesy Harvey Nichols; **27cr** AA/S Montgomery; **28** Courtesy EDF Energy London Eye/British Tourist Authority/James McCormick; **29tl** Courtesy EDF Energy London Eye; **29tr** Courtesy EDF Energy London Eye; **29c** Courtesy EDF Energy London Eye; **30/31** Courtesy Museum of London; **31tr–31cr** AA/J Tims; **32** Ronald Weir/TTL; **33tl–33c** AA/J Tims; **33tr** Courtesy The National Gallery; **34** Courtesy The National Gallery; **35tl** Courtesy The National Portrait Gallery/Andrew Putler; **35tr** AA/J Tims; **35cl** AA/S Montgomery; **35cr** AA/J Tims; **36tl** AA/N Setchfield; **36/37t** AA/M Jourdan; **36/37c** Courtesy Natural History Museum **37r** Courtesy Natural History Museum/Derek Adams; **38/39** Pawel Libera Images/Alamy; **39tr** London Stills; **39cr** AA/M Jourdan; **40** Courtesy Royal Botanic Gardens, Kew/A.McRobb; **41tl** Courtesy Royal Botanic Gardens, Kew/J.Morley; **41tr** AA/B Smith; **41cl** Courtesy Royal Botanic Gardens, Kew/A.McRobb; **41cr** Courtesy Royal Botanic Gardens, Kew/A.McRobb; **42** David Noton/TTL; **43l** AA/S Montgomery; **43r** SJ Images/Alamy; **44l** London Stills; **44/45t** Courtesy St Paul's Cathedral/Peter Smith; **44cr** AA/AA; **45cl** AA/AA; **45r** AA/S Montgomery; **46l** Courtesy Science Museum; **46/47t–46/47c** AA/J Tims; **47** Courtesy Science Museum; **48l** Neil Setchfield/Alamy; **48/49** VIEW Pictures Ltd/Alamy; **49tr** Courtesy Trustees of Sir John Soane's Museum/Derry Moore; **49cr** Nigel Dickinson/Alamy; **50tl** AA/J Tims; **50/51t** The Courtauld Gallery/James Tims; **50/51c** AA/J Tims; **51tr** The Courtauld Gallery/James Tims; **52t–53tr** AA/S Montgomery; **54tl** AA/N Setchfield; **54/55t** AA/J Tims; **54cr–55cl** AA/S Montgomery; **55tr** Courtesy Herzog & de Meuron/Hayes Davidson; **56/57t** AA/C Sawyer; **56cl** AA/T Woodcock; **56/57c** AA/J Tims; **57tr** Courtesy London Duck Tours Ltd; **57cr** AA/J Tims; **58t–59c** AA/S Montgomery; **60/61** Maurice Crooks/Alamy; **61tr** Courtesy Victoria and Albert Museum/Alan Williams; **61cr** Courtesy Victoria and Albert Museum/Richard Waite; **62tl** Tom Mackie/TTL; **62tr–63tr** AA/J Tims; **64** AA/R Mort; **66bl** AA/J Tims; **66br** AA/S Montgomery; **67bl–67br** AA/J Tims; **68b** AA/N Setchfield; **69bl–69br** AA/J Tims; **70b** AA/S McBride; **71b** AA/N Setchfield; **72bl–72br** AA/J Tims; **73bl** AA/S Montgomery; **73br** Courtesy Zoological Society of London; **74bl** AA/S Montgomery; **74br** AA/J Tims; **75b** AA/J Tims; **76bl** AA/P Kenward; **76br** Courtesy Museum of London; **77bl** Courtesy V&A Museum of Childhood/Will Pryce; **78bl–78br** AA/Derek Forss; **79bl** AA/W Voysey; **79br** AA/J Tims; **80** AA/S Montgomery; **82tr** AA/J Tims; **82cl** AA/S Montgomery; **82br** AA/M Jourdan; **83tr** AA/S Montgomery; **83cl** AA/R Turpin; **83br** Courtesy EDF Energy London Eye; **86tr** AA/J Tims; **86cr** AA/S Montgomery; **87b** AA/J Tims; **88tr** AA/N Setchfield; **88cl** Courtesy Museum of London; **89tr** AA/S Montgomery; **89 lower c** AA/W Voysey; **92tr** Courtesy Museum of London; **92cr** Courtesy St. Paul's Cathedral/Peter Smith; **92br** AA/S Montgomery; **93b** Courtesy Transport for London/Hayes Davidson; **94l** Neil Setchfield/Alamy; **94b** The Courtauld Gallery/James Tims; **95tr** AA/J Tims; **95br** AA/J Tims; **98tr** AA/N Setchfield; **98ct** AA/M Taylor; **98br** The Courtauld Gallery/James Tims; **100t** Courtesy The National Portrait Gallery/Andrew Putler; **100cr** AA/J Tims; **101t** London Stills; **101bl** AA/C Sawyer; **104i** AA/J Tims; **104ii** AA/S Montgomery; **104iii** AA/J Tims; **104iv** London Stills; **104v** AA/S Montgomery; **104vi** AA/S Montgomery; **104vii** AA/S Montgomery; **104viii** AA/N Setchfield; **105tr** AA/B Smith; **106l** Courtesy Victoria and Albert Museum; **107tr** AA/J Tims; **107b** AA/S Montgomery; **110i** AA/P Kenward; **110ii** AA/P Kenward; **110iii** AA/T Woodcock; **110iv** AA/J Tims; **110v** Courtesy Victoria and Albert Museum/Morley von Sternberg; **112t** AA/S and O Mathews; **112br** David Noton/TTL; **113t** AA/S and O Mathews; **113cl** AA/W Voysey; **116tr** AA/AA; **116cr** AA/M Jourdan; **116br** Courtesy Royal Botanic Gardens, Kew/A. McRobb; **118** AA/J Tims; **120/121t–120/121ct** AA/S Montgomery; **120/121cb** AA/M Trelawny; **121ct** AA/P Kenward; **121cb** AA/R Turpin; **120/121b** AA/R Strange; **125br** AA/J Tims; **127br** AA/S Montgomery; **128** AA/J Tims; **130/131t** AA/J Tims; **130/131ct** AA/J Tims; **130cb** AA/J Tims; **130/131b** AA/S Montgomery; **131ct** AA/J Tims; **131cb** AA/M Jourdan; **134tl** AA/J Tims; **139tr** AA/R Turpin; **140** AA/J Tims; **142i** AA/AA; **142ii** AA/M Jourdan; **142iii** AA/N Setchfield; **142iv** AA/J Tims; **146bl** AA/N Setchfield; **146br** AA/J Tims; **148tl** AA/N Setchfield; **152** AA/R Mort; **154i** AA/W Voysey; **154ii** AA/J Tims; **154iii** OneOff Travel/Alamy; **154iv** VIEW Pictures Ltd/Alamy; **157b** AA/S Montgomery; **158tl** AA/J Tims; **160** AA/S Montgomery

Every effort has been made to trace the copyright holders, and we apologise in advance for any unintentional omissions or errors. We would be pleased to apply any corrections in a following edition of this publication.

CITYPACK
LONDON

WRITTEN BY Louise Nicholson
ADDITIONAL WRITING BY Sue Dobson
SERIES EDITOR Marie-Claire Jefferies
PROJECT EDITOR Laura Linder
COVER DESIGN Nick Johnston
DESIGN WORK Catherine Murray
INDEXER Joanne Phillips
PICTURE RESEARCHER Wilf Matos
IMAGE RETOUCHING AND REPRO Jacqueline Street

© **AA MEDIA LIMITED 2012**
First published 1996

Colour separation by AA Digital Department
Printed and bound by Leo Paper Products, China

A CIP catalogue record for this book is available from the British Library.

ISBN 978-0-7495-7192-4

Published by AA Publishing, a trading name of AA Media Limited, whose
registered office is Fanum House, Basing View, Basingstoke, Hampshire
RG21 4EA. Registered number 06112600.

A04634
Enabled by Ordnance Survey   This product includes mapping data licensed from
Ordnance Survey® with the permission of the Controller
of Her Majesty's Stationery Office. © Crown copyright 2012. All rights reserved.
Licence number 100021153

Titles in the Series